PLANTS
AND
PLANT LIFE

VOLUME 8
Conifers

MICHAEL ALLABY

GROLIER
EDUCATIONAL

About this Set

PLANTS AND PLANT LIFE *is a ten-volume set that describes the world of plants in all its facets. Volume by volume, you will be introduced to the many different aspects of plant life.*

The first three volumes (1: Roots, Stems, and Leaves, 2: Flowers and Fruits, and 3: Life Processes) explain the basic structure, reproductive methods, and processes of life in flowering plants.

Volume 4 (Plant Ecology) explores the place of plants in the living community of life on Earth, while Volume 5 (Plants Used by People) presents the literally hundreds of plants that have been exploited by people for food, clothing, building, and many other uses.

The final five volumes (6: Algae and Fungi, 7: Mosses and Ferns, 8: Conifers, 9: Flowering Plants—The Monocotyledons, and 10: Flowering Plants—The Dicotyledons) lead the reader on a journey of discovery through the main groups of life that are usually classed as plants. In these volumes the typical and characteristic features of each group and its components are clearly outlined.

Though each volume deals with a distinct aspect of plant life, many of them are interrelated. To help you understand these links, every entry has enlightening cross-references to other entries and volumes. Throughout the set you will also find special short boxed features— entitled "Protecting Our World"—that focus on particular stories of environmental concern.

The whole set is liberally illustrated with diagrams explaining plant processes and structures, with depictions of typical plants and maps showing global distribution. In addition, hundreds of photographs bring the world of plants vividly to life. At the end of every volume there is a useful glossary explaining the technical terms that are used in the text, an index to all the volumes in the set, and finally, a list of other sources of reference (both books and websites). All the plants mentioned in the volume are listed alphabetically by common name, with their scientific names alongside.

Contents

Published 2001 by Grolier Educational, Danbury, CT 06816

This edition published exclusively for the school and library market

Planned and produced by Andromeda Oxford Limited, 11–13 The Vineyard, Abingdon, Oxon OX14 3PX, UK
www.andromeda.co.uk

Copyright © Andromeda Oxford Limited 2001

Project Director: *Graham Bateman*
Editorial Manager: *Peter Lewis*
Art Editors and Designers: *Martin Anderson, Chris Munday, Steve McCurdy*
Editors: *Penelope Isaac, Eleanor Stillwell*
Cartography: *Richard Watts, Tim Williams*
Editorial Assistant: *Marian Dreier*
Picture Manager: *Claire Turner*
Production: *Clive Sparling*
Index: *Ann Barrett*

Originated and printed in Hong Kong

Library of Congress Cataloging-in-Publication Data

Plants and plant life.
    p.   cm.
    Includes bibliographical references.
    Contents: v.1. Roots, stems, and leaves --
v. 2. Flowers and fruits -- v. 3. Life processes
-- v. 4. Plant ecology -- v. 5. Plants used by people
-- v. 6. Algae and fungi -- v. 7. Mosses and ferns
-- v. 8. Conifers -- v. 9. Flowering plants--the Monocotyledons -- v. 10. Flowering plants--the Dicotyledons.
    ISBN 0-7172-9510-9 (set : alk. paper) --
ISBN 0-7172-9518-4 (vol. 8)
    1. Plants--Juvenile literature. 2. Botany--Juvenile literature. [1.Plants--Encyclopedias.
2. Botany--Encyclopedias.] 1. Grolier Educational Corporation.

QK49 .P54 2000
580--dc21
                                    99-056140

Set ISBN 0–7172–9510–9

Volume 8 ISBN 0–7172–9518–4

What Is a Conifer?

SPRUCE, LARCH, PINE, AND FIR are the most abundant trees in the band of forest that stretches across Alaska, northern Canada, Scandinavia, and the Russian taiga. The trees, and others like them, bear their seeds in cones, so they are known as conifers, and the northern forest is said to be coniferous.

As well as their cones, conifers have very characteristic leaves. In many species they are long, narrow, and sharply pointed like needles. Other species have very small, flattened leaves that look like scales. In almost all species—the larches are an exception—the trees do not shed all their leaves at the same time. They are evergreens: plants that remain in leaf throughout the year. Conifers do shed their leaves when they are old, worn out, and have become useless. Depending on the species, conifer leaves last from three to 10 years before being shed. Many conifers have juvenile leaves when they are young. As they mature, they are replaced with adult leaves of a different shape. The floor of a coniferous forest is covered, in most places, with a deep carpet of dead, discarded needles.

From the Arctic to the Tropics

Conifers can grow in climates that are too cold for broad-leaved trees, such as oaks and maples.

They thrive inside the Arctic Circle, but they are not found exclusively in very cold climates. Hemlocks, Douglas firs, redwoods, and cypresses grow much farther south and form magnificent forests in western North America, as well as in China and Japan. Pines grow naturally in both eastern and western parts of the United States and around the shores of the Mediterranean.

Conifers also grow in the tropics. Most are confined to mountainsides, where the climate is cool, but some species grow in the lowlands. New Caledonia, in the South Pacific, has the most diverse conifer population in the world, with 44 species in 14 genera (meaning groups of related species).

Adapted to Survive Drought

What all the conifer habitats have in common is a time of year when the ground is very dry. Conifers can survive a long dry season better than most broad-leaved trees, and it is their leaves that help them.

▶ **Conifer forest in the Rockies. The trees' pyramid shape and tough, springy branches allow conifers to shed snow.**

Like all green plants, conifers make their own food by the process of photosynthesis, using carbon dioxide, water, and energy from sunlight. Oxygen and sugar are the products. Photosynthesis takes place in specially adapted cells in the leaves.

Conifer leaves have a small surface area and are tough; they are covered with a waxy outer skin that makes them waterproof. The leaves have tiny pores—called stomata—that can be opened or closed, allowing gas exchange and water evaporation. Each leaf has only a few stomata, and in many species they are arranged as one or more rows on the underside, visible as white or gray lines. Located on the lower surface of a leaf that is partly folded around them, conifer stomata are sheltered from the drying effect of the wind. Very little moisture is lost through them.

The leaves' toughness and ability to minimize the loss of water mean that they stay on the tree through the driest part of the year. This also allows the tree to carry out photosynthesis whenever it can find enough water in the ground.

In the far north and high on the sides of mountains the ground is often covered with snow throughout the long winter. Water is plentiful, but both above and below the ground it is frozen. Plant roots are able to absorb water only while it is liquid, so ice and snow are of no use to them. Since the water they need is not available to them, the ground is as dry as any desert. The conifers survive; and when the first drips of water signal the coming of spring, they are able to resume their growth immediately because their leaves are still in place.

As well as coping with a lack of water, conifers can also tolerate very wet conditions, and there are some species of juniper, cypress, fir, and pine that grow in swamps or at the edges of lakes and rivers. One example, swamp cypresses, grow in swamps where the ground is permanently waterlogged. They have protrusions from their roots that stick above the surface. Air enters the roots through pores in the protrusions. Roots will die unless they have air for cell respiration.

LIFE CYCLE OF A SCOTS PINE

Mature conifers (1) produce both female and male cones. The female cone (2) consists of many scales (3), each with two ovules. Every ovule (4) has a nucellus (made from unspecialized cells) with a protective structure, the integument, that encloses it completely, except for a single opening called the micropyle. In the nucellus there is a megaspore mother cell (the female reproductive cell).

A male cone (5) consists of hundreds of microsporophylls (modified leaves), each bearing a microsporangium, or pollen sac (6). Pollen mother cells (7) inside the microsporangia divide by meiosis (reduction division) to produce microspores, each with a single set of chromosomes. In meiosis a cell with two sets of chromosomes divides twice to produce four cells, each with one set of chromosomes. The microspores develop into pollen grains.

A pollen grain (8) is enclosed in two layers—the exine (outside) and intine (inside)—and is attached to two air sacs. Inside the grain are the prothallial, tube, and generative cells. The generative cell divides to form two sperm cells. After pollen release the male cone dies.

Wind carries the pollen grains; some land on female cones. There (9), a pollen grain is drawn through the micropyle into the ovule. This is pollination and the female cone scales close up (10). The pollen grain matures into the male gametophyte (the structure containing sperm cells) and starts to grow a pollen tube (14). It digests its way through the nucellus, a process that takes a year in most species.

During that year the megaspore mother cell undergoes meiosis, producing four megaspores (11), only one of which survives and germinates (12). It divides repeatedly, developing into the female gametophyte (a structure containing female reproductive cells). Two or three archegonia (female sex organs) develop inside the female gametophyte (13); each contains one egg.

The pollen tube reaches the female gametophyte as the eggs are ready to be fertilized. Two male nuclei (sperm cells) move down the pollen tube (14). One is injected into an egg and unites with it. This is fertilization: the fertilized egg is called a zygote. Usually only one zygote survives. At fertilization the cone has grown and is green (15).

The zygote cell begins to divide, forming a proembryo

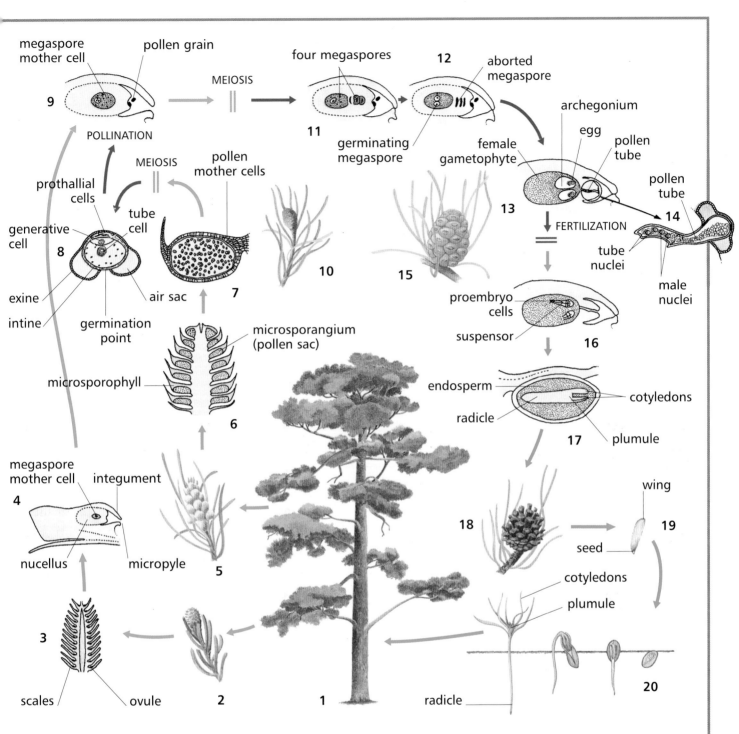

megaspore mother cell

pollen grain

MEIOSIS

four megaspores

12

aborted megaspore

9

POLLINATION

11

germinating megaspore

archegonium

egg

pollen tube

MEIOSIS

pollen mother cells

female gametophyte

pollen tube

prothallial cells

13

generative cell

tube cell

8

exine

intine

germination point

air sac

7

FERTILIZATION

tube nuclei

male nuclei

14

microsporangium (pollen sac)

10

15

proembryo cells

suspensor

16

microsporophyll

endosperm

cotyledons

6

radicle

plumule

17

megaspore mother cell

integument

wing

4

18

19

nucellus

micropyle

seed

5

cotyledons

plumule

3

scales

ovule

2

1

radicle

20

(16), which separates to produce the cells that will be the embryo, and the suspensor, which attaches the embryo to the ovule and supplies it with nutrients. The embryo (17) is the new plant. It is the start of the sporophyte generation (a stage when all the cells have two sets of chromosomes).

The embryo has the start of a root (radicle), a shoot (plumule), and seed leaves (cotyledons). It is surrounded by endosperm, a food supply that will sustain the plant until it can begin photosynthesis.

The ovule, now a seed, is contained within a seed coat. It is carried on one of the scales of the now brown female cone (18). When it is released (19), its "wing" helps carry it away from the parent tree. On the ground the seed germinates (20).

See Also | POLLEN 2 16 | THE CELLULAR BASIS OF REPRODUCTION 2 40 ◉

▼ ► Unlike most conifers, yews produce their nutlike seeds in a fleshy cup called an aril (below). More typically, each spring the Austrian pine (right) produces clusters of small, red, female cones at its shoot tips, and yellow male cones farther back. Male cones die once pollen is released. The next year pollinated female cones grow, turning first green, then brown as the seeds they contain mature.

Shedding Snow

Snow and ice are heavy, and conifers are better equipped to bear the weight than most broad-leaved trees. Many have a single, straight trunk with branches that are long near the bottom and progressively shorter up the tree's height, giving the tree its pyramid shape. In some species the branches droop a little, and in all conifers the stem and branches are fairly flexible: they can bend a long way before breaking. As snow accumulates on the tree, the branches bend under the weight until they have bent so far that the snow starts to slide off. As soon as this happens, the weight is reduced, and the branches spring back to their former position, shedding the remaining snow as they do so.

The conical shape of a conifer is a result of the way the trees grow. New cells are produced at the tip of the trunk and at the tip of each branch. The tip of the trunk grows fastest, since that is where cell division is most intense. As the trunk grows, branches develop behind the leading shoot (usually at the tip of the trunk). The youngest branches are the shortest, and they are at the top of the tree. Branches below them are older and therefore longer, with the longest at the bottom.

Beneath the Bark

An outer layer of dead tissue forms the bark, which protects the trunk and branches from diseases and pests. Beneath the bark are the living tissues that perform specialized functions. Phloem cells conduct sugars from the leaves to all parts of the plant. They are cylindrical cells, laid end to end to form tubes called vessels. Beneath the phloem there is another layer of cells that carries water containing dissolved nutrients from the roots. In conifers the cells through which water travels are known as tracheids. They are long, with tapering ends that overlap and give the tree its strength. Broad-leaved trees have a different type of water-carrying cell that is more efficient but gives less support. Broad-leaved trees have fewer water-carrying cells, but they are embedded in a number of tough fiber cells to give strength. Most of the living parts of the trunk and branches of a conifer consist of tracheids. As a result, the wood of most conifers is softer than that of most broad-leaved trees. Wood from conifers is classified as "softwood," and wood from broad-leaved trees is "hardwood."

Ancient Trees

The first conifers evolved about 300 million years ago, during the Carboniferous Period, and the ancestry of some of those living today can be traced back a long way. Monkey puzzle and redwood trees belong to families that have existed for 195 million years, and the pine family is 135 million years old.

Today the conifers are classified as the phylum Coniferophyta (or Pinophyta). There are about 50 genera and more than 550 species. They include the tallest trees in the world and the oldest. Coast redwoods can grow to a height of 390 feet (120 m), and some bristlecone pines are up to 5,000 years old.

LIFE OF A DOUGLAS FIR

After 30–40 years (a) lower branches start to fall, and the tree can be used to make paper. At 50–60 years (b) the trunk can be used as a pole. At 100 years (c) it can be used for building timber. Full-grown (d), the tree is up to 330 feet (100 m) tall. After several centuries (e), branches start to fall, bark peels, and the trunk starts to rot. Eventually, the upper branches drop (f), and the trunk is rotten. The dead tree falls down (g).

See Also | *CELL TYPES AND TISSUES* **1** *18* | *STEMS* **1** *28* | *LEAVES* **1** *38* ◉

Pines *PINUS*

PINE TREES ARE TYPICALLY TALL AND PYRAMID-SHAPED; but when the wind dries one side of the tree more than the other, a pine can develop a stunted shape. They are often grown in parks and gardens; lodgepole pine and eastern white pine are among the most popular ornamental species.

Scalelike leaves grow in a spiral on young pine shoots. As the shoot grows, the young leaves fall off and are replaced by the adult leaves. The leaves, or needles, are about 5 inches (13 cm) long and usually grow in groups of two, three, or five, but occasionally only one or as many as eight. At their base all the needles in a group are surrounded by a sheath made from up to 12 scales that formerly enclosed the leaf bud. Adult leaves have been discovered to last for five or more years before they are discarded.

Male and female cones are both found on the same tree. The male cones resemble catkins. Mature female cones vary in size according to the species, but some are quite large. Those of the ponderosa pine are up to 6 inches (15 cm) long, while those of the pitch pine and eastern white pine can be 8 inches (20 cm) long, and the sugar pine has cones measuring up to 20 inches (50 cm) long. Apart from size, the female cones differ in that the scales of the cones point outward and often end with a projecting point.

Resin, Soft Pines, and Hard Pines

Like most conifers, pines produce resin. Resin is a sticky liquid that dissolves in alcohol but is insoluble in water. It solidifies on exposure to air; and when a conifer is injured, the tree exudes resin to protect the wound. Resin is produced in channels called resin ducts. In some conifers ducts develop only if the tree is injured, but in pines they are present all the time. The resin helps preserve the wood once harvested, making it suitable for outdoor use.

▶ Pines grow in many parts of the world. Scotch pine, Corsican pine, Aleppo pine, and cluster pine are among those native to Europe and the region around the Mediterranean. Bhutan pine grows to a height of 165 feet (50 m) and has prickles on the cone that break easily. It comes from the Himalayan region. The ponderosa pine, beach pine, eastern white pine, and Monterey pine are all species that grow in North America.

PINES
Genus: *Pinus*

FAMILY: Pinaceae

NUMBER OF SPECIES:
Nearly 200

DISTRIBUTION: Northern temperate regions as far south as Central America, the West Indies, Sumatra, and Java

ECONOMIC USES: Important for timber and pulp, also sources of turpentine and resins, and edible seeds; many grown as ornamentals

Beach pine ▶
(*P. contorta*)

cones often curved

young cone

Corsican pine ▼ ▶
(*Pinus nigra* var.
maritima)

male cone

twisted leaves

Bhutan pine ▲
(*P. wallichiana*)

Eastern white pine ▶
(*P. strobus*)

Ponderosa pine ▼
(*P. ponderosa*)

Bark of ▶
Monterey pine
(*P. radiata*)

leaves in bunches
of two, four,
or five

Aleppo pine ▶
(*P. halepensis*)

leaves in
bunches of
two or three

cone scales
open to shed leaves

Bark of Ponderosa pine ▲
(*P. ponderosa*)

leaves grow
in clusters

Cluster pine ▲
(*P. pinaster*)

cones not symmetrical

leaves in
bunches of five

▲ Bhutan pine (*P. wallichiana*)

▲ Monterey pine (*P. radiata*)

See Also CELL TYPES AND TISSUES **1** 18 | GROWING BIGGER **1** 46 | THE WORLD'S BIOMES **4** 36 👁

Pines are the most important of all timber-producing conifers. Once impregnated with a preservative, the wood is used to make railroad ties and telephone poles. The lodgepole pine, which is the inland variety of the beach pine, earned its name because it was used in the building of Native American lodges. Pine timber is used in all types of construction.

Some species contain more resin than others. This difference is reflected in the wood and causes pines to be classed as "soft" or "hard." Soft pines contain much less resin than hard pines, and their wood is soft, with a close grain. The eastern white pine and sugar pine are soft, and so are the stone and foxtail pines, although they are not important for their timber. Stone pines grow in the mountains and are valued for binding soil and preventing erosion.

Hard pines have much heavier, coarser wood. The pitch pine, native to the southeastern United States, is a hard pine that grows to 120 feet (37 m). It is the most important source of lumber in the southern states. Its wood is very durable and can be polished. Ponderosa pine, which can reach a height of 200 feet (61 m), is the most widespread North American species. Its wood is easily worked, and the tree is commercially important, especially in the Pacific

◀ A Scotch pine tree standing by itself will have a domed shape. When grown close together in forests, Scotch pine trees have straight trunks and a crown of branches near the top.

▶ The bristlecone pine of North America is the most long-lived tree in the world. Some trees are believed to be up to 5,000 years old.

states. Monterey pine is native to parts of the California coast, but it is grown for timber in many parts of the world.

Loblolly pine, which grows naturally over most of the eastern United States, is also called the "old-field" pine because it often appears on abandoned farmland. Its cones have particularly sharp spines. It grows quickly, so is useful as a screen, and its timber is used extensively.

The Long-lived Bristlecone Pine

Many types of tree usually live for a few centuries, but some pines are a notable exception. In the dry hills of the western United States there is a slow-growing tree called the hickory pine. It is conical in

shape and up to about 30 feet (10 m) tall, with dense foliage and branches that turn up at the ends. Its leaves have been calculated to live for up to 20 years. It is remarkable because the tree itself lives for about 2,000 years.

In the same area its close relative, the bristlecone pine, is even more remarkable. It can live for up to 5,000 years, which means trees that are now nearing the end of their lives were seedlings when the Babylonian Empire was being established, and Egyptians were developing their hieroglyphic method of writing. When a bristlecone pine dies, its wood can take a further 4,000 years to decay. Scientists have found wood from bristlecone pines that is estimated to be 8,200 years old.

See Also | *SURVIVING EXTREMES* **3** *42* | *TIMBER* **5** *44* | *WHAT IS A CONIFER?* **8** *4* 👁

Spruces *PICEA*

WITH THEIR TALL, CONICAL SHAPE, horizontal or drooping branches, and dark foliage, spruces are very distinctive. They are of great economic importance. Although widely grown for ornament, nowadays spruces are the principal source of wood for pulping to make paper. This book may very well be made from spruce.

Originally from northern California and Oregon, Brewer's spruce is one of the most popular ornamental species because of its appearance. Its branches droop, curving upward toward the tips, and have shoots with leaves hanging from them.

Spruces can be recognized by their needles. They grow singly, rather than in bunches like those of pines, and they do not arise directly from the twig but from a small wooden "peg" on the twig surface. If you pull the needle away, the peg will come with it,

leaving a scar on the twig; but if the needle falls naturally, the peg will be left behind. So, if the needles grow from pegs, and there are also pegs without needles on the twig, the tree is a spruce.

Male and female cones are borne on the same tree. Male cones are red or yellow, about one inch (2.5 cm) long, and appear on shoots that grew the previous year. Immature female cones are green or purple, often stand erect, and when mature they hang down from the branches. Their scales open as soon as their seeds are

ready to be released, but the scales do not fall from the cones.

Exposed Sites and Dark Forests

Most spruce species will grow in cold, wet ground, and provided the soil is deep enough for their roots to gain a secure anchorage, they can withstand strong winds. This allows them to grow high in the mountains and to be planted commercially on exposed hillsides.

Where spruces grow in forests, their conical shape and dense foliage combine to cast a deep shade. They also shelter the ground from the wind, so there is very little air movement. A spruce forest can be a dark, gloomy, still, and rather eerie place.

Sitka Spruce

Sitka spruce is probably the most widely cultivated of all spruce species. It takes its name from the town of Sitka on the western coast of Alaska, and it grows naturally along the western coast of North America as far south as California.

SPRUCES

Genus: *Picea*

FAMILY: Pinaceae
NUMBER OF SPECIES: 34
DISTRIBUTION: Cool regions of the Northern Hemisphere, as far as the Arctic Circle, and mountains as far south as the Tropic of Cancer
ECONOMIC USES: Timber and wood for pulp; Christmas trees; bark for tanning; turpentine; pitch; resin to make chewing gum; boiled shoots and leaves to make beer; some grown as ornamentals

▶ In much of Europe the main species used for Christmas trees are spruces. Here is a plantation of Norway spruces being grown in the Channel Islands.

▼ Spruces have long, cylindrical female cones that hang from the branches. The most important American timber species include the Sitka spruce. Colorado spruce is grown for ornament.

▼ Sitka spruce
(*Picea sitchensis*)

spruce needles grow singly

cone scales are open but retained

▼ Serbian spruce
(*P. omorika*)

Himalayan spruce ▶
(*P. smithiana*)

◀ Colorado spruce
(*P. pungens*)

▲ Norway spruce (*P. abies*)

Serbian spruce (*P. omorika*) ▲

See Also | *STEMS 1* 28 | *ZONATION 4* 26 | *TIMBER 5* 44 👁

◀ Spruces that have attractive shapes and brightly colored foliage are often cultivated for parks and gardens. Above left: Colorado spruce, cultivar 'Koster,' has silvery-blue leaves. Below left: Caucasian spruce cultivar 'Aurea' produces bright golden leaves in spring that turn green after six weeks. Left: Norway spruce cultivar 'Pendula' has attractively drooping branches.

Varieties that grow in the north are adapted to short summers and long, dark winters. When planted in Europe, they stop growing at the end of July. European foresters prefer to plant seeds from Sitka spruces that grow in California; the trees continue to grow until December. Sitka spruces can grow to 200 feet (60 m); but when they are grown commercially, they are felled before they reach this size.

Engelmann, Norway, and Other Spruces

The Sitka spruce is widely cultivated in North America as well as in Europe. The Norway spruce rivals it in importance in Europe, as does the slower-growing Engelmann spruce in the United States. Engelmann spruce occurs naturally in the Rocky Mountains at elevations up to 12,000 feet (3,660 m). Norway spruce is native to most of northern and central Europe, including the taiga in Russia.

Norway spruce is traditionally used as a Christmas tree in Britain (but not in North America). Sitka spruce is also used, but its needles have very sharp points, which can make it difficult to handle.

Red spruce grows on the eastern side of North America, from Canada to North Carolina. It has bright-green leaves and can grow to 100 feet (30 m) tall. White spruce and black spruce grow throughout northern North America, up to the Arctic treeline. White spruce has gray bark and bluish-green needles, and can grow to a height of 60 or 70 feet (18 to 21 m). Black spruce has dark-green needles. Popular as ornamentals, there are dwarf varieties of both.

Colorado spruce can be found from Wyoming to Colorado. It can reach 165 feet (50 m) and has a conical shape. Its leaves are stiff, thick, and have sharp points. They are gray-green in color and covered with a bluish wax. The blue Colorado spruce is a variety with blue-gray leaves that is a very popular ornamental. Serbian spruce is narrow, its upper part

▶ Acid rain has contributed to damage in some European forests by making the soil acidic. That makes it more difficult for trees to absorb nutrients.

spire-shaped. It is native to south-eastern Europe but especially common in Serbia and Bosnia. Himalayan spruce, found from Afghanistan to Nepal, is similar, though less spirelike.

Spruce Wood

All the spruces produce wood that is soft, odorless, very pale in color, and often called white-wood. It is easy to work, has an even texture, and can be polished. Thin sheets of it resonate to the vibration of a plucked or bowed string, so spruce is used to make guitars, violins, cellos, and other stringed instruments. It is also used to make packing cases and boxes.

White spruce and black spruce are used for their lumber. Engelmann spruce and Norway spruce are important sources of lumber too. Spruce wood is not very durable for outdoor use, but this can be remedied: it absorbs preservative well, so can be used for fencing and telephone poles.

Today a large amount of spruce timber is made into board, including chipboard and hard-board. The biggest market of all, however, is for making paper.

PROTECTING OUR WORLD

ACID RAIN

Air pollution has combined with the effects of drought, disease, and pest attacks to harm trees in some parts of North America and Europe. The damage has been blamed on "acid rain." It is rain containing dilute sulfuric and nitric acid from the burning of coal and oil. Ozone, from smog, also caused harm. The acid affected some types of soil in ways that made it more difficult for tree roots to absorb nutrients. Not all tree species were affected to the same extent, but some American spruces and firs suffered badly. Pollution controls have reduced acid rain, but it will take many years for some soils to recover.

Firs *ABIES*

IN NORTH AMERICA THE TREES THAT ARE DECORATED as part of the Christmas celebrations are either balsam or Fraser firs. They are usually conical or cylindrical in shape and symmetrical. Their handsome appearance means they are often grown for ornament in parks and large gardens.

Fraser fir can grow to 40 feet (12 m), and balsam fir to 50 feet (15 m), so they are both fairly small trees. Variety *hudsonia* is a dwarf form of the balsam fir that reaches no more than 2 feet (60 cm) and does not produce cones. Christmas trees are usually young trees that are cut when they reach a suitable height.

Some fir trees grow to be extremely tall, however, a fact that is reflected in their common names. In natural forests the noble fir can grow to a height of 260 feet (80 m), and the giant fir can reach 330 feet (100 m), although in cultivation they seldom exceed 150 feet (45 m) and 200 feet (60 m).

Recognizing a Fir

Fir trees are sometimes called silver firs to distinguish them from Douglas firs, which they resemble. The two kinds of fir can be easily identified since they differ in their needles, buds, and cones.

The needles of silver firs grow singly, not in bunches, and directly from the twig, rather than on a small peg or shoot. Along the surface of each twig there are small, round scars. The scars mark the places where needles used to grow. If the scars feel quite smooth, then the tree is a silver fir.

Buds of silver fir are plump, short, and often feel sticky because they exude resin. They are very distinctive and quite different from the buds of Douglas firs. The cones are even more distinctive. Those of silver firs are erect, either standing upright or projecting at right angles from the stem. They never hang downward. When the seeds are mature, the cone disintegrates, leaving behind a central spike, called the "fir candle," that falls after about a year. The presence of fir candles is a sure sign the tree is a silver fir.

The noble fir is particularly easy to recognize. The gray-green to gray-blue needles on its side twigs are swept upward, and the scales of its cones end in long spikes that point downward. The tree is sometimes called the "feathercone" fir. Once the tree is more than 20 feet (6 m) tall, however, the cones are borne only on the topmost branches. In Denmark the noble fir is the preferred species for a Christmas tree.

FIRS

Genus: *Abies*

FAMILY: Pinaceae

NUMBER OF SPECIES: 39

DISTRIBUTION: temperate regions of the Northern Hemisphere, especially in the mountains, and in Central America

ECONOMIC USES: important source of timber; resins; Canada balsam; Alsatian turpentine; Christmas trees; many grown as ornamentals

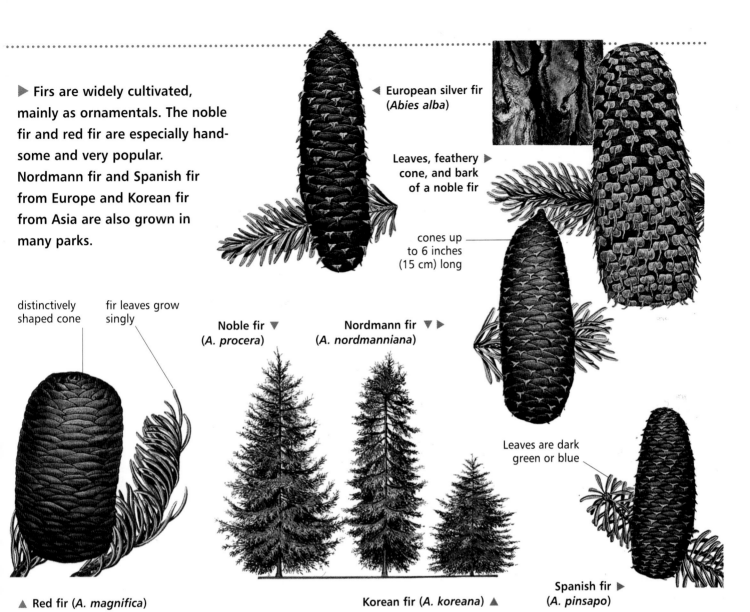

Firs are widely cultivated, mainly as ornamentals. The noble fir and red fir are especially handsome and very popular. Nordmann fir and Spanish fir from Europe and Korean fir from Asia are also grown in many parks.

European silver fir (*Abies alba*)

Leaves, feathery cone, and bark of a noble fir

cones up to 6 inches (15 cm) long

distinctively shaped cone

fir leaves grow singly

Noble fir ▼ (*A. procera*)

Nordmann fir ▼ ▶ (*A. nordmanniana*)

Leaves are dark green or blue

▲ Red fir (*A. magnifica*)

Korean fir (*A. koreana*) ▲

Spanish fir ▶ (*A. pinsapo*)

Commercial Cultivation

The European silver fir is one of the best-known species. It is a tall tree, sometimes reaching a height of 150 feet (45 m), and is widely cultivated. Originally it came from central and southeastern Europe, and it still forms extensive forests in the mountains of southern Germany and France, and in Italy. It is no longer grown commercially in Britain because it succumbed to attacks from an insect pest that was accidentally introduced from eastern Europe and caused "silver fir dieback."

The giant fir is a native of British Columbia, Oregon, and Idaho. It grows fast; and while it is young, it can tolerate shade. This allows its seedlings to be planted among other trees, which provide shelter. In the wild it can grow to 330 feet (100 m), but in cultivation it only grows to about 165 feet (50 m). It is resistant to frost and to most diseases and insect attacks.

The Pacific, or Cascade fir, can grow to 260 feet (80 m) in the wild, although it seldom grows to more than 100 feet (30 m) in cultivation. It is found in western North America from southern Alaska to northern California, but especially in the Cascade and Olympic mountain ranges. It can suffer attacks from aphids.

The red fir, from the region between southern Oregon and northern California, can reach 120 feet (35 m). It is somewhat

PROTECTING OUR WORLD

SAVING NATURAL FOREST

Coniferous forest covers a vast area of the world's landmass, but the global demand for soft-wood timber is so large that without careful management, some of the most valuable parts of it could be cleared. Most of the areas in Canada are now protected. Elsewhere, forests are allowed to regenerate after trees have been felled, and plantations are supplying an increasing amount of timber. Approximately two trees are planted each year for each tree felled, so the Canadian forest is expanding. Forests are also protected in Scandinavia and Russia, although there is a danger that where valuable parts of the taiga are accessible, they will lose a number of trees.

cylindrical in shape, with a thick trunk. Its leaves are four-sided. They are a bright gray-blue on the upper side and have bands of gray on the underside, and its cones are barrel-shaped, golden-green in color, and up to 10 inches (25 cm) long. The white fir is another large tree, up to 130 feet (40 m) tall and occasionally taller. It grows naturally from Oregon to New Mexico.

Timber and Resin

Timber from fir trees is very similar to that from spruces and, like spruce, is often called white-wood. It is used in construction, telephone poles, and, since it has no obvious odor, for making boxes and packing cases, as well as for pulping to make paper. It is not very durable but can be treated with preservative for outdoor use. Fir is considered to be of inferior quality to spruce and pine, so it is less widely grown for commercial timber production outside the areas where it occurs naturally. In ancient Greece timber from the Greek fir trees was used to build ships.

The value of the fir lies not so much in its wood as in its resin. There is so much of it that in summer it often collects in blisters on the bark. Resin from the European silver fir is purified and sold as Alsatian, or Strasbourg, turpentine. It is used as an ingredient in some of the very best varnishes, and it is also used medicinally, in inhalants.

Resin from the balsam fir, a native of central and eastern Canada and the northeastern United States, is used to make Canada balsam, also known as balsam of fir and Canada turpentine. It is a pale yellow liquid consisting of resin dissolved in a volatile oil that evaporates on exposure to air. When the resin sets, light passes through it in almost exactly the same way it passes through glass. This means that it has a similar refractive index, and this makes Canada balsam useful for mounting specimens on microscope slides and in cementing glass to make lenses.

Ornamental Firs

Firs are even more important as ornamental trees. The Korean fir has leaves that are dark green on the upper side and silver on the underside. A native of South Korea, it is a small tree, some-times a shrub, that is now widely cultivated in other countries.

Nordmann fir is rather cylindrical in shape and grows to about 165 feet (50 m), but there are dwarf varieties, including ones with bright golden-yellow leaves. The species is from the Caucasus region (between the Black and Caspian seas) and northern Turkey, and thrives in places that have hot summers. Spanish fir, which is a smaller tree with gray-blue leaves, tolerates alkaline soils.

▲ A Christmas tree at Rockefeller Center in New York. Balsam firs are the most popular species at Christmas time in the United States.

◄ Spring growth of the giant fir is an attractive pale green.

Hemlocks *TSUGA*

WHEN THE LEAVES OF HEMLOCK ARE CRUSHED, they have an earthy smell that is said to resemble the smell of the hemlock plant, a quite unrelated and very poisonous weed. That is how the trees earned their name. In fact, hemlock trees are handsome, pyramid-shaped trees that are grown for their timber and as ornamentals.

Hemlocks are not difficult to identify: their leaves are narrow but flat and vary in length along the shoot. The leaves have a short stalk and grow in two rows on either side of the shoot.

Male cones are almost spherical and no more than 0.25 inch (6 mm) across. They are usually red, but can be yellowish-white, and are borne at the tips of side shoots. The female cones are small —less than 1 inch (2.5 cm) long. When mature they hang down and remain on the tree for some years after releasing their seeds.

Hemlock Species

Western hemlock, also known as Prince Albert's fir and the hemlock fir, is from northwestern coastal regions of North America. It is widely grown, and its timber is exported to many parts of the world. Its wood is considered far superior to that of other types of hemlock and comparable to pine and spruce. The tree has been known to grow to more than 210 feet (65 m). As it grows, the growing tip of the seedling has a very distinctive droop.

Canada hemlock, from eastern North America, is a much smaller tree. It is a popular ornamental species, with many cultivated varieties. Some of them, such as 'Cole's Prostrate,' are only about 12 inches (30 cm) tall and are grown for ground cover. Others have been bred for the color of their leaves, which are of various shades of green, some with tips of silver. Mountain hemlock, native to the western coast from Alaska to California, has bluish or gray-green leaves and reddish bark and shoots. It grows to 50 feet (15 m), but there is also a slow-growing dwarf variety that is popular for its foliage.

Carolina hemlock sometimes reaches a height of 70 feet (20 m) but is usually smaller. It is a conical shape with red-brown bark and dark-green leaves. Widely grown as an ornamental, it occurs naturally from Virginia to Georgia in the southern Alleghenies.

Chinese hemlock is a bigger tree, growing up to 165 feet (50 m) tall. It is usually conical in shape and has attractive bark. Two Japanese species, the northern and southern Japanese hemlocks, both grow to about 25 feet (8 m). The northern has orange shoots and slightly orange bark. The southern has dark-gray bark and buff shoots.

HEMLOCKS

Genus: *Tsuga*

FAMILY: Pinaceae

NUMBER OF SPECIES: 10

DISTRIBUTION: North America and eastern Asia

ECONOMIC USES: timber, wood pulp; bark for tanning; some grown as ornamentals

22 HEMLOCKS

▲ Male cones of western hemlock shedding their pollen.

Uses for Hemlock

The smaller species of hemlock are suitable for hedging, while all the dwarf varieties can be grown as bonsai trees. Hemlocks tolerate shade well, so they are not harmed by being crowded together in a hedge.

Hemlock wood is pale brown and darker than pine or spruce. Ladders were formerly made from it, and it is used in construction. It is also used to make boxes and packing cases and for pulping to make paper.

The bark, called tanbark or hemlock bark, is used in North America for tanning leather. The resin, sometimes called Canada pitch, is also used commercially.

▶ Leaves, bark, and female cone of western hemlock, and leaves, cone, and mature tree of Canada hemlock.

◀ Young western hemlock trees in a natural forest. They will remain small until an old tree falls, providing a space that the tree can grow to fill. This group is in Soleduck Valley, in Olympic National Park, Washington State.

leaves in two rows

young cone

Western hemlock ▶
(*Tsuga heterophylla*)

mature cone

Canada hemlock ▲
(*T. canadensis*)

See Also | POLLEN **2** 16 | SUCCESSION **4** 24 | PINES **8** 10 | SPRUCES **8** 14

Douglas Firs *PSEUDOTSUGA*

DOUGLAS FIRS ARE TALL, PYRAMID-SHAPED TREES WHEN YOUNG that become broad and conical when mature. They are grown as ornamentals in many public parks and open spaces. A Scottish botanist called David Douglas (1798–1834) sent the first seeds from a Douglas fir to Britain in 1827, and the tree was named after him.

Douglas did not discover the tree, however. Another Scottish botanist, Archibald Menzies (1754–1842), first saw and recorded it in 1791, and is remembered in the scientific name for the species, *menziesii*.

The tree they saw represents all the species in the genus, so they are known collectively as Douglas firs and are broadly similar to each other. Their leaves grow from very small stalks. When the needles fall, they leave small, round scars on the twig, like those on silver fir, but on Douglas firs the scars are very slightly raised. When crushed, the leaves have a smell somewhat like citrus fruit.

At the tip of each twig there is a pointed bud that is highly distinctive and quite different from the buds of silver fir; it is covered in brown, papery scales. Male cones resemble catkins. The egg-shaped female cones are borne on the same tree as the male cones. They are 2–4 inches (5–10 cm) long and hang downward. Each scale on the cone has a straight, papery covering (a bract) that ends in three points. No other conifer has cones like this.

American and Asian Douglas Firs

The Douglas fir tree that Douglas and Menzies saw can reach a height of 330 feet (100 m). In 1895 one was felled in British Columbia that measured 436 feet (135 m). It is truly a giant. It grows naturally in western North America, from British Columbia to California.

Commercially, its timber is the most important in North America; and although Douglas firs account for half of all the trees in forests where they occur, there is concern that the trees are being harvested faster than they can be replaced.

The timber is often marketed overseas as Oregon pine or Colombian pine because of its resemblance to pine. It is used for telephone poles, flagpoles, railroad ties, railroad wagons, building boats, and in construction. Since the wood is available in very large pieces, it is also used in the building of bridges.

DOUGLAS FIRS

Genus: *Pseudotsuga*

FAMILY: Pinaceae

NUMBER OF SPECIES: 6

DISTRIBUTION: western North America, Mexico, and eastern Asia

ECONOMIC USES: an important source of timber, plywood, and pulp; also grown as ornamentals

▶ **A Douglas fir growing in a park. The handsome trees are often grown as ornamentals in public places.**

The other North American species is the large-coned Douglas fir, found in southwestern California. It is a smaller tree, easily identified by its cones. They are 4–7 inches (10–18 cm) long.

Both American species have leaves with pointed tips. The leaves of the Asian species are distinguished by a notch at the tip. Japanese Douglas fir, from southeastern Japan, is up to 100 feet (30 m) tall. Its cones are only 1–2 inches (2.5–5 cm) long. The Chinese Douglas fir, from western China, has slightly larger cones. It grows to about 65 feet (20 m).

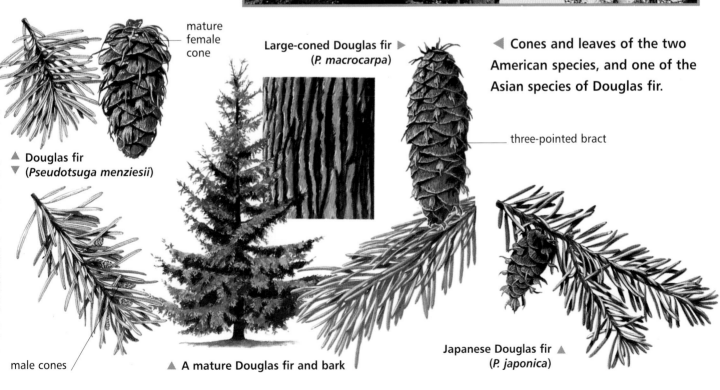

mature female cone

Large-coned Douglas fir ▶
(*P. macrocarpa*)

◀ **Cones and leaves of the two American species, and one of the Asian species of Douglas fir.**

three-pointed bract

▲ **Douglas fir**
▼ **(*Pseudotsuga menziesii*)**

male cones

▲ **A mature Douglas fir and bark**

Japanese Douglas fir ▲
(*P. japonica*)

Larches   *LARIX*

LARCHES ARE AMONG THE MOST BEAUTIFUL OF CONIFEROUS TREES, not only in shape, but also for their fall colors. Unlike almost all other conifers, larches are deciduous, shedding their leaves every fall. The leaves turn red or yellow before they drop from the trees, creating a splash of color among the evergreen trees.

Early in the year, when they first appear, the leaves are bright emerald green. They darken through the summer before changing color in the fall. In winter the tree has no leaves at all, except while they are very young. Larches retain all their leaves through their first winter, and for a few years after that they do not shed the leaves at the tips of their twigs.

At the tip of each twig the leaves grow singly. Elsewhere, they grow in whorls made up of clusters of 20–30, from very short shoots. Leaves vary in length according to the species, but larch leaves are generally more than one inch (2.5 cm) long. The short shoots, with their leaf clusters, are arranged spirally along the twig. When the leaves fall, the short shoots remain as small, woody knobs. Larches can be identified by their short shoots even when the trees are leafless.

Cones

Male cones are spherical or egg-shaped and pink or yellow. Mature female cones are erect.

Unusually for a conifer, the cones mature within one year. When they are young, they are green, pink, or white. At this stage they are sometimes called larch "roses." The cones turn pale brown as they mature. They are cylindrical, oval, or conical in shape and quite small. Once fertilized, two seeds develop under each cone scale, each with its own "wing."

The cones of Sikkim larch, a tree from eastern Nepal, Sikkim, and Tibet, are 2.5–4 inches (6–10 cm) long, but those of most larches are no more than 1.5 inches (4 cm) long.

Larch Species

Various species of larch are the most abundant trees in the Eurasian taiga. In Russia larches alone occupy more than 1 million square miles (2.6 million sq. km). They grow on mountainsides, the European larch being found at elevations up to 5,000 feet (1,525 m).

European larch is one of the most widely cultivated species. A native of northern and central

---

LARCHES

Genus: *Larix*

FAMILY: Pinaceae

NUMBER OF SPECIES:
9–14 depending on classification

DISTRIBUTION: cool regions of the Northern Hemisphere

ECONOMIC USES: important source of timber; bark used for tanning; resin used medicinally and in veterinary medicine

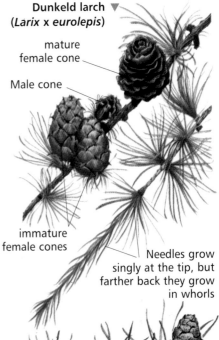

◀ Immature female larch cones, showing their pink-edged scales.

Dunkeld larch ▼
(*Larix* x *eurolepis*)

mature female cone

Male cone

immature female cones

Needles grow singly at the tip, but farther back they grow in whorls

Leaves, cone, ▲ ▶ and bark of European larch

Daurian larch ▼ (*L. gmelini*)

▼ European larch (*L. decidua*)

Japanese larch (*L. kaempferi*) ▲

▶ European larch is a tall, conical tree. Japanese larch is smaller and broader, with branches that curve upward. The two species have hybridized to produce the Dunkeld larch. Daurian larch is the predominant species in the eastern part of the Eurasian taiga.

Europe, and also of Siberia, it is a conical shape, sometimes with drooping branches that turn up at the tips, and it grows to a height of about 115 feet (35 m). There are many cultivated varieties. The variety 'Pendula' has long, drooping branches, known as a weeping habit. 'Corley' is a dwarf variety, growing to about 3 feet (1 m) high and as wide as it is tall.

Tamarack, also called hackmatack and eastern larch, is the most wide-ranging North American species. It occurs naturally from Pennsylvania northward to Labrador and northwestward from there to the Yukon and Alaska. It is up to 65 feet (20 m)

See Also | *SURVIVING EXTREMES* **3** *42* | *THE WORLD'S BIOMES* **4** *36* | *TIMBER* **5** *44* 👁

PROTECTING LARCHES

When plants or animals live crowded together, diseases can quickly spread among them. This can cause severe problems for trees grown on plantations, and larches are prone to a variety of pests and diseases that are difficult to control. Where the trees are over-crowded, and the soil is wet, they are prone to larch canker, caused by a fungus. It makes the tree useless and may kill it. Honey fungus can also prove fatal. Several insects feed on larch leaves or shoots and can retard the growth of a tree or even kill it. Pesticides must sometimes be used to prevent infections from spreading.

tall. Like the European larch, it grows rapidly for the first 25 to 50 years; then its growth slows, and the tree matures when it is 100–200 years old.

Western larch is the tallest of all the larches. It can grow to a height of 180 feet (55 m), with a trunk that is 4 feet (1.2 m) in diameter. A native of western North America, western larch grows in valleys and on mountainsides at elevations from 2,000 feet (610 m) to 7,000 feet (2,100 m) in British Columbia, Washington, Oregon, and Idaho.

Siberian larch is the most abundant species in the western part of the taiga. To the east of the Yenisei River there is a transitional zone where there are hybrids of Siberian and Daurian (or Dahurian) larches, and beyond that Daurian larches predominate. Daurian larches, which grow to about 100 feet (30 m) tall, are able to live farther north than any other species of larch. They have shallow roots that can draw water from the uppermost layer of soil, above the permafrost (the layer that remains permanently frozen). Their name is taken from the Dagur (or Daur) people of northern Manchuria.

Japanese larch is widely grown in Europe and North America. In about 1904 Japanese larches were planted on the estate of the Duke of Atholl, at Dunkeld, Scotland. By chance, male cones of the European larch pollinated female cones of Japanese larch. This gave rise to a hybrid larch that is usually known as Dunkeld larch. Its appearance is very variable, but it grows faster than either of its parents, thrives in poorer soil, and can tolerate more exposure to wind and rain. It is also resistant to larch canker, one of the most serious diseases of larches, caused by a fungus.

Uses for Larch

Larch timber is strong and durable. Most wood can be treated with preservatives nowadays, but traditionally larch was used outdoors for gates, fences, roof shingles, telephone poles, and for the exterior planking on fishing boats—for which a special grade of "boat-skin" larch was used.

Because they grow so quickly, larches are also used as "nurse trees." Broad-leaved trees are planted among young larches. As they grow, the larches protect their broad-leaved neighbors from the wind. By the time the broad-leaved trees are big enough to suffer from the shade cast by the larches, the larches are ready to be felled.

Resin obtained by tapping larch trees is refined to make Venice, or larch, turpentine. It is used in veterinary medicines to treat skin irritations and parasites. In summer larch leaves exude a white, sweet substance called larch manna that people used to rub on their chests to relieve bronchial ailments.

▶ Larches in their fall colors. This group is in the Black Forest, Germany.

Cedars *CEDRUS*

THE CEDAR OF LEBANON SYMBOLIZES POWER AND A LONG LIFE in the Middle East. Perhaps the most beautiful of all conifers, its distinctive shape is familiar since it features in many pictures of the lands of the eastern Mediterranean. Like all cedars, it is an evergreen tree grown for ornament. Cedars grow best in a mild climate.

In the United States cedars are cultivated mainly in California and the southern states, although some hardy varieties are grown as far north as New England.

There are only four species of true cedars, and scientists suspect they may really be local varieties of a single species. Despite this, there are up to 70 trees that are unrelated to true cedars but are nevertheless called cedars.

Cedar leaves are needles, 0.25–2 inches (0.5–5 cm) long depending on the species. They are borne in clusters of 10–45 on short shoots that are able to grow into long shoots, with the whorl of leaves at the tip. The leaves last for about a year.

Cedars do not produce seeds until they are 40 or 50 years old. Male cones are then produced from September to November. They are erect, oval, or conical, brown, and up to 2 inches (5 cm) long. Female cones are erect, barrel-shaped or cylindrical, and 2–4 inches (5–10 cm) long. They take two or three years to mature, then shed their scales as the seeds are released.

The Four Species

The most famous species is the cedar of Lebanon, a native of the eastern Mediterranean from Lebanon to Turkey and the mountains of Syria. It grows to a height of 130 feet (40 m). At first the tree grows vertically and has a conical shape; but as it matures, the top of the tree flattens, giving it a domed shape. Its long branches grow upward but after a short distance become horizontal. They give the tree its characteristic layered appearance. The tree is then approximately as broad as it is tall and requires ample space if it is to grow healthily and be seen at its best. There is a cultivated variety, 'Sargentii,' which can be grown as a shrub.

The Cyprus cedar is from the mountains of Cyprus in the eastern Mediterranean. Smaller than the cedar of Lebanon, it usually grows to about 40 feet (12 m) and is a similar shape.

At the western end of the Mediterranean the Atlantic cedar grows in the Atlas Mountains of Algeria and Morocco at elevations from 4,000 feet (1,220 m) to 6,000 feet (1,830 m). It grows to the size of the cedar of Lebanon but is a quite different shape. An Atlantic cedar is pyramid-shaped, and its branches point upward. Because they do not become

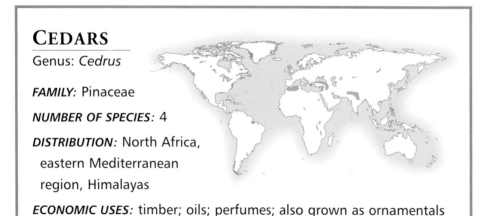

CEDARS

Genus: *Cedrus*

FAMILY: Pinaceae

NUMBER OF SPECIES: 4

DISTRIBUTION: North Africa, eastern Mediterranean region, Himalayas

ECONOMIC USES: timber; oils; perfumes; also grown as ornamentals

◀ Deodar with male cones and immature female cones.

▼ Atlantic cedar (*Cedrus atlantica*)

leaves in clusters

Deodar (*C. deodara*) ▼

Immature female cone

▼ Cone and foliage of the cedar of Lebanon

▲ Cedar of Lebanon (*C. libani*)

▲ A blue-leaved variety of the cedar of Lebanon, with an immature female cone.

▲ The cedar of Lebanon is instantly recognizable by its layered appearance. Atlantic cedar is a popular ornamental. The deodar is commercially important in India.

horizontal, the tree does not develop the layered appearance of the cedar of Lebanon or the Cyprus cedar.

The deodar, also called the Himalayan cedar or the Indian cedar, is by far the biggest. It can reach a height of 200 feet (60 m), and the diameter of its trunk can be 40 feet (12 m). Its name, deodar, is Hindi and means "divine tree." It is an important timber tree in India.

Cedar wood is used to make furniture and in construction. Solomon's temple was built from the wood of the cedar of Lebanon. The blue Atlas cedar, which is the variety *glauca* of the Atlantic cedar, has vividly blue foliage. There are many cultivated varieties. 'Aurea,' another variety of Atlantic cedar, has golden foliage when it is young, which turns green later.

See Also | *LEAVES 1 38* | *OIL CROPS 5 30* 👁

Redwoods
SEQUOIA, METASEQUOIA, SEQUOIADENDRON

SOME REDWOOD TREES ARE SO IMPRESSIVE they are given individual names. The General Sherman tree is one of them. Located in the Sequoia National Park, California, it is believed to be the most massive tree in the world—although it is not the tallest. It stands 272.4 feet (83 m) tall, and near its base the diameter of its trunk is 32.2 feet (10 m). It weighs about 2,200 tons (2,000 tonnes).

The General Sherman tree is very old. It grew from a seed that germinated more than 3,000 years ago. It belongs to the species known as the big tree, or giant redwood. The trees grow naturally only on the western slopes of the Sierra Nevada. They are all massive; they can grow to more than 330 feet (100 m), with a trunk 34 feet (10.5 m) across.

Big trees are conical in shape. The leaves are narrow, wedge-shaped, and 0.5 inch (1.2 cm) long. They grow alternately, point forward, and completely enclose the shoot.

The male cones turn yellow in spring when they mature. They are about 0.2 inch (0.5 cm) long. Female cones mature in their second year. Then they are woody, oval in shape, and 2–3 inches (5–8 cm) long.

Coast Redwood

The tallest redwoods belong to a different species; the coast redwoods, which are found in the coastal regions of California and Oregon. They rarely occur more than 25 miles (40 km) from the coast or at elevations higher than 3,500 feet (1,100 m). Some specimens can grow up to 395 feet (120 m), although most are much smaller.

Coast redwoods are conical in shape or straight-sided and are slimmer than big trees. Their branches are horizontal or slightly drooping. Grown in forests, they lose their lower branches, leaving a bare trunk with a conical crown.

REDWOODS

Genera: *Sequoia*, *Metasequoia*, *Sequoiadendron*

FAMILY: Taxodiaceae

NUMBER OF SPECIES:
Sequioa 1, Metasequoia 1, Sequoiadendron 1

DISTRIBUTION: *Sequoia* and *Sequoiadendron* in western North America; *Metasequoia* in central China

ECONOMIC USES: *Sequoia* a valuable timber tree; other species valued as ornamentals

▲ Dawn redwood growing in a park, where its shape is well displayed.

◀ A magnificent big tree growing as an isolated specimen, where its lower side branches are retained. In forests lower branches are dropped (see right).

They have two types of leaves. On main shoots they are oblong, arranged spirally around a shoot, and have a tip about 0.2 inch (0.5 cm) long that curves toward the twig. On side shoots leaves like curved needles are 0.2–0.7 inch (0.5–1.8 cm) long.

Male cones are brownish-green and quite tiny. The biggest are only 0.06 inch (0.15 cm) long. Female cones measure up to 1 inch (2.5 cm) long.

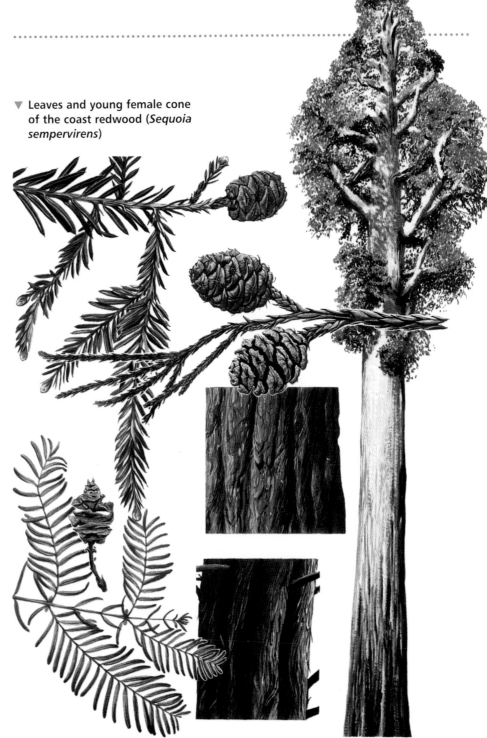

▼ Leaves and young female cone of the coast redwood (*Sequoia sempervirens*)

Leaves, mature female cone, ▲ and bark of the dawn redwood (*Metasequoia glyptostroboides*)

The big tree (*Sequoiadendron* ▲ *giganteum*): its leaves, young and mature female cones, and its deeply furrowed bark

Dawn Redwood

The third member of the group is the dawn redwood. Unlike the other redwoods, it is deciduous,

▲ Each of the three redwood genera has a single living species, while Metasequoia also has fossil representatives.

See Also | STEMS **1** 28 | GROWING BIGGER **1** 46 | PLANTS UNDER THREAT **4** 44 ◉

losing its leaves every fall. Before they drop, the leaves turn a golden or red color. In their natural habitat some dawn redwoods grow to 130 feet (40 m) tall, and in cultivation they reach about 65 feet (20 m). They are slender, conical trees.

Until 1941 scientists believed the dawn redwood had been extinct for about 26 million years; only fossils of it were known. In that year, however, living specimens were discovered in Hubei and Sichuan provinces of China. Seeds were collected in 1947, and the first dawn redwoods were planted in the west in 1948.

The leaves are flat, with parallel edges, and are arranged in pairs along either side of the shoots. They are up to 0.75 inch (2 cm)

▼ **Big trees being felled in California. Felling is under strict environmental control.**

long. Male cones occur in clusters of two to five. They are brown, spherical, and up to 0.5 inch (1.5 cm) long. Female cones are cylindrical in shape, about 1 inch (2.5 cm) long, and each cone is borne on a stalk up to 1.5 inches (4 cm) long. Although they produce cones, cultivated dawn redwoods fail to set seed, possibly because male cones do not produce fertile pollen. The trees are grown from cuttings.

They grow fast, often at a rate of 3.3 feet (1 m) a year for the first 10 years, after which they grow more slowly. This rapid rate of growth may lead to dawn redwoods being grown commercially.

Bark and Timber

All the redwoods have very thick, soft bark. It is reddish-brown in color, fibrous, deeply furrowed, and it resists attack by insects, fungi, or fire. On fully grown big

▶ **A named tree, this is the Grizzly Giant big tree in the Mariposa Grove, in Yosemite National Park, California.**

trees and coast redwoods the bark is 12 inches (30 cm) thick, and it is dense: you can punch it quite hard without hurting your fist.

Only the coast redwood produces valuable timber. That from the big trees is brittle, so is used for fences and roof shingles, and dawn redwoods are not available in sufficient numbers. Coast redwood timber, however, is soft, fine-grained, and strong. It is suitable for all kinds of carpentry and construction, as well as for railroad ties and telephone poles.

All three species are grown in parks and gardens. There are cultivated varieties of coast redwoods that have bluish-green and pale-green leaves. Other varieties produce trees of different shapes.

PROTECTING OUR WORLD

MANAGING THE REDWOODS

Coast redwoods yield such valuable timber that for many years mature trees were felled faster than new trees could grow. The result was severely depleted redwood groves. Most of the remaining redwood groves now lie inside national or state parks and forests, where felling is controlled. That protection is backed up by conservationists, who still protest when trees are threatened by logging companies. The forests now contain enough young redwood trees that the coast redwood has been saved from extinction in its natural habitat.

Swamp Cypresses *TAXODIUM*

FOUND IN SWAMPS AND AT THE EDGES OF RIVERS, swamp cypresses can survive where the soil is waterlogged and their roots are permanently submerged. They are not confined to wet habitats, though, and grow just as well on dry, well-drained land. Trees grown as specimens for ornament are usually planted in very wet sites.

Plant roots must be able to obtain air. Root cells will die if they are unable to release energy from the reaction called respiration, in which oxygen combines with carbon. The carbon is found in sugars made during photosynthesis. Plants growing on dry land find the air they need in the soil in the spaces between soil particles. When the land is submerged, water pushes all the air out of the soil, and most plants die.

Surviving below Water

Swamp cypresses survive by producing "knees." They are loops from the horizontal roots that project upward so the top of each loop is above the surface of the water. The bark on the knees contains many small pores through which air can enter. Once inside the root, the air diffuses to all parts of the root cells.

The main roots join the trunk some way above the water. They grow away from the trunk, forming structures resembling buttresses (they are called buttress roots), which help support the tree. Just below the surface of the mud they branch into the smaller, horizontal roots.

Leaves and Cones

Conical trees up to 165 feet (50 m) tall, swamp cypresses are often rounded at the top. They produce two types of shoot. One type bears leaves arranged in two rows on opposite sides but produces no buds. They are shed, usually in the fall. The other type of shoot is persistent, has leaves arranged all around it, and produces buds from which new leaves grow to replace those shed.

The leaves are pale green and narrow, with a sharp point. The leaves on shoots that are shed turn reddish-brown before falling. The Montezuma, or Mexican, cypress is evergreen in Mexico, but specimens grown in cooler climates shed all their leaves in the fall.

Male cones form in groups. Female cones take one year to mature. They are then spherical and about 1 inch (2.5 cm) in diameter.

Big and bald cypresses

The Montezuma cypress is cultivated in Mexico for its timber and its resins, which are used medicinally. It is long-lived: there is one popular specimen, in the village of Santa Maria del Tule,

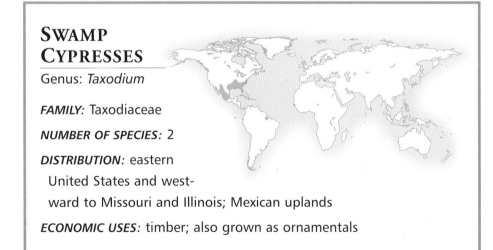

SWAMP CYPRESSES

Genus: *Taxodium*

FAMILY: Taxodiaceae

NUMBER OF SPECIES: 2

DISTRIBUTION: eastern United States and westward to Missouri and Illinois; Mexican uplands

ECONOMIC USES: timber; also grown as ornamentals

Montezuma cypress (*T. mucronatum*) ▼

Bald cypress ▶
(*T. distichum*)

female cone

Bark and leaves of ▲
the pond cypress
(*T. distichum* var.
imbricarium)

Bald cypress ▲
(*T. distichum*)
with knees

near the city of Oaxaca. The Spanish conquistador Hernando Cortés described it in about 1520. It was old then, and it is still there. A source of local pride and called the Tule Tree, or *El Gigante*, it is believed to be more than 2,000 years old. It is also large: its trunk is 56 feet (17 m) in diameter. However, it is really three trees that have fused together. The tree is a popular

▲ Bald cypresses in a swamp in Florida. Note the distinctive buttress roots that help support the trees.

tourist attraction, but its survival is threatened by the expansion of the village. This has increased the demand for water and is depriving the tree of its supply.

The bald cypress is the most widely cultivated species. As well

▲ The bald and Montezuma cypresses are similar, but the latter is semi-evergreen. Leaves of the pond cypress are awl-shaped. It was once classed separately.

as being a popular ornamental, with several varieties, it is grown for its soft, durable timber. It is used to make packing cases, railroad ties, fences, and items of garden furniture.

See Also | ROOTS **1** 22 | PHOTOSYNTHESIS **3** 4 | RESPIRATION **3** 10 👁

Monkey Puzzle Trees *ARAUCARIA*

IT IS IMPOSSIBLE TO MISTAKE THE MONKEY PUZZLE TREE for any other species. It grows wild in central Chile and in the Andes, on the border between Chile and Argentina. Seeds were taken back to Europe in 1795 and again in 1844, and the tree became a familiar sight in 19th-century public parks and suburban gardens.

The monkey puzzle is a large tree, up to 100 feet (30 m) tall. As the tree ages, its lower branches fall, leaving a straight trunk with a domed crown of long branches. The branches curve upward, which gives the tree a striking appearance.

Its leaves grow all around the branches and overlap each other, pointing away from the trunk. Each leaf is triangular, with a sharp point. Leaves last for 10–15 years and are 2 inches (5 cm) long and 1 inch (2.5 cm) wide at the base. Young leaves are bright green; older ones are dark green.

Male cones form in cylindrical clusters about 4 inches (10 cm) long. Female cones are oval, about 6 inches (15 cm) long, and take two to three years to mature. The seeds are edible as Chile nuts.

Bunya-bunya

From Queensland, the bunya-bunya is a fast-growing tree that can reach 165 feet (50 m). Its main branches are horizontal, but smaller ones hang down. The tree tends to lose its lower branches as it grows older. Its leaves are similar to those of the monkey puzzle, but smaller. Male and female cones are usually borne on separate trees. The egg-shaped female cone is about 12 inches (30 m) long, 9 inches (23 cm) wide, and weighs up to 11 pounds (5 kg). Its seeds are edible.

Hoop Pine

Hoop pines grow in Australia and New Guinea. Their name refers to the red-brown bark, which cracks into horizontal bands around the trunk as new bark replaces it. The branches are horizontal; most of the small branches concentrate at the ends of main branches.

They are conical or cylindrical trees, up to 230 feet (70 m) tall. Young trees have leaves that are either oval or like needles, with sharp points and up to 0.7 inch (1.8 cm) long. On older trees leaves of this type also grow on shoots that lack buds. Shoots with buds on older trees have crowded, overlapping, scalelike leaves that are up to 0.3 inch (0.8 cm) long.

Male cones are up to 3 inches (7.5 cm) long and hang in clusters. Female cones are oval and about 4 inches (10 cm) long.

MONKEY PUZZLE TREES

Genus: *Araucaria*

FAMILY: Araucariaceae

NUMBER OF SPECIES: 19

DISTRIBUTION: southwestern Pacific, especially New Caledonia, New Guinea, New Hebrides, Norfolk Island, and Queensland, and in South America from southern Brazil to Chile and western Argentina

ECONOMIC USES: timber, especially for plywood; ornamentals

Paraná and Norfolk Island Pine

The paraná pine, from Brazil and Argentina, is up to 115 feet (35 m) tall and has softer leaves than the monkey puzzle tree. Its branches grow around the trunk in whorls of four to eight.

Norfolk Island pine, a conical tree that can reach a height of 230 feet (70 m), has spherical cones up to 4 inches (10 cm) in diameter. It occurs naturally only on Norfolk Island in the South Pacific, and it is widely grown for ornament. In cooler climates its seedlings can be grown indoors.

Timber from members of this family is soft, resinous, and easy to work. It is used for most kinds of carpentry, to make boxes, and for pulp. Wood from the klinki pine of New Guinea (also in the South Pacific) is peeled away in layers and used to make plywood. The tallest of all tropical trees, its height has been recorded at 292 feet (88.9 m).

▼ Norfolk Island pine is a popular ornamental in warm climates. Note how the side branches point upward.

▶ Monkey puzzle trees are seen at their best where there is enough space to display them. This young specimen will grow into a very big tree.

Monkey puzzle tree (*Araucaria araucana*). Bark, leaves, mature female cone, and a full-grown tree

◀ Far left: Monkey puzzle trees have very distinctive bark and leaves.
Left: Norfolk Island pine has two types of leaf—tightly-packed on old shoots, and more widley spaced on young shoots.

◀ Norfolk Island pine (*A. heterophylla*)
▲ and (above) its awl-shaped leaves from a young shoot

See Also | *LEAVES* **1** 38 | *TIMBER* **5** 44 | *PLANTS IN HORTICULTURE* **5** 48 👁

Cypresses
CUPRESSUS/CHAMAECYPARIS/x CUPRESSOCYPARIS

IN ANCIENT TIMES THE ITALIAN CYPRESS SYMBOLIZED DEATH. Also known as the funeral cypress, its wood was used to make the sarcophagi, or caskets, in which the mummified bodies of important Egyptians were buried. To the Greeks the tree was sacred to Pluto, god of the underworld; statues of their gods were made of its wood.

The cypresses include two genera, known as true cypress (*Cupressus*) and false cypress (*Chamaecyparis*), and the Leyland cypress (x *Cupressocyparis*), which is a hybrid of the two. Both true and false cypresses are evergreen trees with a conical shape. Most produce commercially valuable timber.

Some false cypresses have needlelike leaves when they are young, but all mature cypresses have very small leaves that overlap and hug the twigs. They look like scales, up to 0.25 inch (6 mm)

long, with tips that point away from the trunk of the tree. In the young shoots of false cypresses the leaves are in pairs that are opposite each other and all in the same plane, so the shoot appears flattened. In true cypresses, and mature shoots of false cypresses, they completely enclose the twig.

Male and female cones are borne on different branches of the same tree. The male cones of false cypresses are oval or spherical and up to 0.25 inch (6 mm) long; those of true cypresses are rather smaller, and they are borne at the

tips of shoots. Mature female cones of true cypresses are spherical or egg-shaped and usually more than 0.4 inch (1 cm) long. False cypress mature female cones are spherical and less than 0.4 inch (1 cm) across.

True Cypresses

Monterey cypress is conical when young but spreads when it is old, developing almost a layered structure. It occurs naturally only in Monterey County, California. Its leaves have a lemon scent when crushed. The tree grows to a height of 80 feet (25 m), but there are cultivated varieties that are much smaller.

There are two varieties of the Italian cypress. One spreads its branches horizontally. The other has a very narrow, conical, or cylindrical shape, with many of its branches pointing upward, parallel to the trunk. It is a striking tree that can grow to 165 feet (50 m), although most specimens are much smaller.

Several true cypresses are natives of North America, in

CYPRESSES

Genera: *Cupressus,*
Chamaecyparis,
x *Cupressocyparis*

FAMILY: Cupressaceae

NUMBER OF SPECIES: 13–24 *Cupressus,* depending on classification; 7 *Chamaecyparis*

DISTRIBUTION: western North America from Oregon to Mexico, Mediterranean region, western Asia, western Himalayas, southern China, Japan

ECONOMIC USES: timber; toiletries; also grown as ornamentals

◀ Monterey cypress in New Zealand, showing its natural spreading shape. In cultivation it is tall, pyramid-shaped, and grows rapidly.

▼ Distinguishing features of some familiar cypresses.

▼ Leaves and mature female cone of (top) the Italian cypress (*Cupressus sempervirens*) and (below) the Monterey cypress (*C. macrocarpa*)

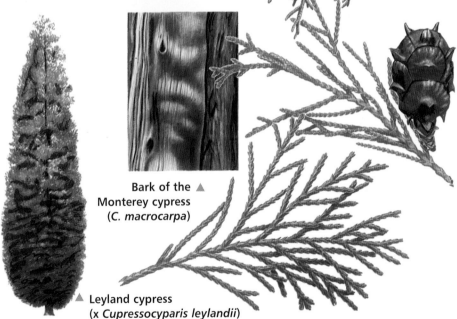

Bark of the ▲
Monterey cypress
(*C. macrocarpa*)

▲ Leyland cypress
(x *Cupressocyparis leylandii*)

addition to the Monterey cypress. The rough-barked Arizona cypress, found from Arizona to New Mexico, grows to about 80 feet (25 m) and has rough, reddish-brown bark. The smooth cypress, which occurs in the southwestern United States, is sometimes mistakenly classed as the same species as the rough-barked cypress, but is actually a species in its own right. It grows in central Arizona and earns its name from its smooth, reddish-purple bark. It is a conical tree up to 60 feet (18 m) tall.

The baker cypress, from Oregon and northern California, has gray or reddish-gray bark and grows to about 50 feet (15 m).

The Guadalupe cypress, from southern California, has red-brown bark in the shape of small flakes. It is conical when young, becoming more oval later. Also

from California, the Gowen cypress is a conical or cylindrical tree up to 30 feet (10 m) tall.

Despite its name, the cedar of Goa is a true cypress and comes

not from Goa, in India, but from Mexico to Guatemala. It has spreading branches, often drooping downward at the ends, and grows to about 100 feet (30 m).

False Cypresses and Leyland Cypresses

The Lawson cypress, a native of the western United States, is the best known false cypress. It is a narrow, conical, or spire-shaped tree up to 165 feet (50 m) tall, with branches that bend downward at the tips. The male cones are brick red; the female cones, up to 0.5 inch (1.3 cm) across, are wrinkled and brown or bluish-green. There are many ornamental varieties, including some that grow to only 6 feet (2 m) tall.

The Alaska cedar grows naturally in western North America from Alaska to Oregon. It is a conical tree up to 130 feet (40 m) tall. Its branches hang downward at the tips. The characteristic has been exaggerated in the ornamental variety 'Pendula,' which has an open crown and foliage that hangs from the branches. White cedar, a tree up to 80 feet (25 m) tall, grows in the eastern United

States. It has dark gray-green or bluish leaves.

Hinoki cypress, from Japan, is a broadly conical tree up to 130 feet (40 m) tall. There are many varieties, some low-growing and suitable for ground cover.

The Formosa cypress, from Taiwan, has leaves that smell of rotten seaweed when they are crushed. It is a big tree, sometimes as much as 210 feet (65 m) tall and with a trunk 25 feet (7.6 m) in diameter. There are

▲ Leyland cypress trees being grown close together to form a hedge.

Foliage, female cones, and ▲
bark of Lawson cypress
(*Chamaecyparis lawsoniana*)

◀ A few of the many cultivated varieties of the Lawson cypress, including those with golden foliage and weeping foliage.

▼ Foliage, with female cone, and bark of Alaska cedar. Peeling bark is typical

A fully grown Alaska cedar ▲
(*Chamaecyparis nootkatensis*)

forests of Formosa cypress, and a Taiwanese subspecies of Hinoki cypress, at elevations of 7,500–10,800 feet (2,300–3,300 m) in the mountains of Taiwan. The Formosa cypress is so valuable for its timber, however, that trees have been felled faster than they can be replaced, and the species is in danger of extinction.

The Leyland cypress, a very fast-growing cypress that is a cross between the Monterey cypress and Alaska cedar is thought to have been developed in the late 19th century in England. Seedlings were raised from the hybrid, and there are now many other ornamental varieties.

▲ The seven species of false cypresses belong to the genus *Chamaecyparis*. Two examples from North America are: right, the Alaska cedar; and left, the narrow, spire-shaped Lawson cypress.

See Also | PLANTS UNDER THREAT **4** 44 | TIMBER **5** 44 👁

Arborvitae *THUJA*

THE ROMANS NAMED THIS TREE ARBORVITAE, which is Latin for "tree of life." They believed that its resin had medicinal value. The two American species are often called cedars, although they are not true cedars. Western red cedar was the tree most often used by Native Americans to make totem poles; it is now grown extensively for timber.

Arborvitae trees are sometimes conical but more usually pyramid-shaped. Their leaves are small, scalelike, and diamond- or wedge-shaped. Leaves growing on young shoots are arranged in pairs on opposite sides of the shoot, giving the shoot a flattened shape. The tips of the twigs feel stout and fleshy to the touch. The leaves grow around the older shoots, completely enclosing them, and point away from the trunk.

Male and female cones are borne on the same tree. The male cones are small, egg-shaped, and grow at the tips of the youngest shoots. Female cones are solitary, erect, and variable in shape, measuring in the range 0.4–1 inch (1–2.5 cm) long.

American Species

Western red cedar is a conical or cylindrical tree native to western North America, which can grow to a height of 200 feet (60 m). When bruised, its leaves have a strongly aromatic scent. Its timber resists the weather well and is used to make roof shingles, boats, ladders, and the "cedar" frames of greenhouses. Its trunks were most often used by Native American Indians to make totem poles.

American arborvitae, also called white cedar, is a much smaller tree, growing up to 65 feet (20 m) in height. It grows naturally in eastern North America and prefers colder climates. Its soft, fragrant wood is used to make fences, and the trees are often grown to provide screening, and as windbreaks. The tree has a rounded shape with spreading branches, and the bark is orange-brown. Its leaves each have a prominent raised dot—in fact a gland—on the underside. The leaves are yellowish-green on the upper side, paler and rather gray on the underside, and they turn brown in winter.

Both western red cedar and white cedar are popular ornamental species, with many varieties that differ in size, shape, and the color of their foliage.

Asian Species

Asian arborvitae species come originally from Korea, Japan, and China. Korean arborvitae is sometimes a small, conical tree up to

---

ARBORVITAE

Genus: *Thuja*

FAMILY:
Cupressaceae

NUMBER OF SPECIES: 6

DISTRIBUTION: North America, eastern Asia

ECONOMIC USES: timber; bark fibers for stuffing upholstery; oils used medicinally; many grown as ornamentals

30 feet (9 m) tall, but is otherwise found growing as a sprawling shrub. Its leaves are diamond-shaped on the young shoots and triangular on the main shoots. They are bright green on the upper side and silver on the underside.

Japanese arborvitae is a tree up to 60 feet (18 m) tall. The undersides of its leaves have white, approximately triangular markings, and the ends of its young shoots are not very flattened.

One of the Chinese species is found in the mountains of north-eastern Sichuan province and is called the Sichuan arborvitae. It is not cultivated, and little is known about it.

The other is the oriental arborvitae, a tree up to 33 feet (10 m) tall that is found in northern and western China. It is usually conical in shape and has fibrous, red-brown bark. Several varieties with yellow or golden foliage are grown as ornamentals. When its female cones are young, their scales are fleshy. This, and the fact that their seeds have no wings, distinguishes the species from other members of the genus, so it is usually placed in a genus of its own, *Platycladus*.

▶ **Among the most widely grown species are: Top: American arborvitae. Middle: western red cedar. Bottom: Japanese arborvitae.**

◀▼ **Arborvitae trees are popular as ornamentals. Many are suitable for small gardens, such as the dwarf varieties of oriental arborvitae (left) and 'Collyer's Gold,' a cultivar of the western red cedar (below).**

▼ American arborvitae (*Thuja occidentalis*)

leaf detail

▼ Western red cedar (*T. plicata*)

leaf detail

leaf detail

The bark, foliage, and female ▲ cones of Japanese arborvitae (*T. standishii*)

▲ American arborvitae (*T. occidentalis*)

See Also | *FIBERS* **5** *34* | *MEDICINAL PLANTS* **5** *42* | *TIMBER* **5** *44* ◉

Junipers *JUNIPERUS*

JUNIPERS ARE EXTENSIVELY CULTIVATED. The French name for juniper berries is *genièvre*. This became "genever" in Dutch and was shortened by the English to "gin," giving a name to the alcoholic drink that is flavored with juniper berries. Some junipers are called "cedars." They include the pencil cedar of eastern and central North America: pencils used to be made from its wood.

Junipers have two types of leaves. Narrow, pointed, juvenile leaves grow either in pairs on either side of the twig or in threes. Some species, including the common juniper, bear only juvenile leaves, but most species also have adult leaves. They are small, scalelike, overlapping, and grow all around the shoot, completely enclosing it.

Juniper "berries" are mature female cones. They take two or three years to develop, at which point they consist of three to eight fleshy scales fused along their edges to produce spherical berries that are up to 0.5 inch (1.5 cm) across. They often have a bluish color and eventually turn black. Depending on the species, each cone contains one to 12 indigestible seeds. Birds eat the cones, distributing the seeds in their droppings. Common juniper cones are used for flavoring.

Male and female cones are usually borne on different plants, but in some species on different branches of the same plant. The male cones are yellow, spherical, or egg-shaped and are up to 0.25 inch (0.6 cm) across.

Common Juniper and Chinese Juniper

Common juniper is a shrub or a cylindrical or egg-shaped tree that grows to a height of about 40 feet (12 m). Found throughout the Northern Hemisphere, its leaves grow in pairs or in threes. They are 0.5 inch (1.3 cm) long, bluish-green in color, with sharp points.

There are many cultivated ornamental varieties of common juniper: 'Compressa' is one of the most popular. It grows very slowly into a narrow, cylindrical tree to about 30 inches (76 cm) tall. There are also varieties that grow across the ground and varieties with golden foliage.

Chinese juniper is a popular garden plant. It can be found in the Himalayas, Mongolia, China, and Japan, and in its natural habitat it is a conical tree up to 65 feet (70 m) tall. Most of the cultivated varieties are much smaller than this but retain the natural shape of the tree.

JUNIPERS

Genus: *Juniperus*

FAMILY:
   Cupressaceae

NUMBER OF SPECIES: 50

DISTRIBUTION: throughout most of the Northern Hemisphere, from the tundra regions inside the Arctic Circle to the mountains of tropical Africa and Central America

ECONOMIC USES: timber; pencils; oils used in polishes and toiletries; "berries" used for flavoring; also grown as ornamentals

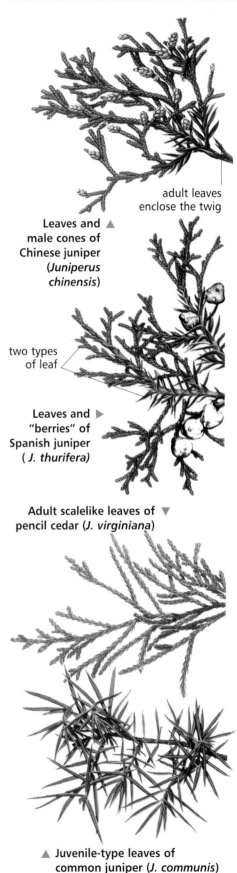

Leaves and ▲
male cones of
Chinese juniper
(*Juniperus
chinensis*)

adult leaves
enclose the twig

two types
of leaf

Leaves and ▶
"berries" of
Spanish juniper
(*J. thurifera*)

Adult scalelike leaves of ▼
pencil cedar (*J. virginiana*)

American Junipers

Ashe juniper is one of several North American species. Native to the southeastern states, it grows either as a shrub or as a spreading tree 20 feet (6 m) tall.

Alligator juniper, from the southwestern United States and Mexico, is a tree that grows to a height of 65 feet (20 m). It is also grown as an ornamental. Rocky Mountain juniper is a shrub or a tree up to 50 feet (15 m) tall. There are several ornamental varieties, many with blue-green leaves and some with branches that hang down in a weeping shape.

Pencil cedar, from eastern and central North America, is conical or spreading in shape, up to 100

▲ **Western juniper growing among granite boulders in the Sierra Nevada Mountains, California.**

feet (30 m) tall. It is cultivated as an ornamental but also has commercial uses: its wood is resistant to insects, and it is used to make mothproof chests. Its oil, called cedar-wood oil, is used in polishes and soap. The wood from this tree, and from the Bermuda cedar, is used to make pencils.

▶ **The most popular ornamental species are the common juniper and Chinese juniper. Pencil cedar is also grown for its wood and oil.**

▲ Juvenile-type leaves of
common juniper (*J. communis*)

See Also │ *DISPERSAL OF FRUITS AND SEEDS* **2** *36* │ *BEVERAGES* **5** *40* 👁

Yews *TAXUS*

MEDIEVAL LONGBOWS WERE MADE from the hard, durable, and flexible wood of the yew tree. The female cones are in the form of bright red berries, the flesh of which is the only part of the plant that is not extremely poisonous. Eating yew leaves, seeds, or twigs can be fatal.

Although the single seed inside each yew berry is extremely poisonous, the poison is released only if the seed is crushed. When a bird eats a berry, the seed passes through its digestive system undamaged and causes no harm.

The scarlet fleshy covering is called an aril. As the nutlike seed ripens, the aril grows to enclose it. It remains open at the end, like a cup attached to the twig, with the seed visible inside. Male and female cones are borne on separate plants. The aril is different from the usual female cone, and the wood and leaves have no resin canals. Both features make yews

▶ An Irish yew. Mature yews found in churchyards can be up to 1,000 years old.

different from all other conifers.

Yew leaves are narrow, with parallel sides, and often darker on the upper side. They are arranged approximately spirally on shoots that grow upward and usually in two rows along horizontal shoots. So-called artichoke galls (close clusters of leaves) are caused by infection with the yew gall midge.

Yew Species

English or common yew occurs throughout Europe, North Africa, and western Asia. It is a spreading, rounded tree that can reach a height of 65 feet (20 m), with leaves 0.75–1.25 inches (2–3 cm) long. Farmers do not allow them to grow where livestock could be poisoned, but yews are often seen in churchyards.

Since the foliage is very dense, English yews can be trained and cut into almost any shape over a number of years. This skilled practice is known as topiary. Cultivars of yews can also be used

YEWS

Genus: *Taxus*

FAMILY: Taxaceae

NUMBER OF SPECIES:
5–10 depending on classification used

DISTRIBUTION: temperate regions of the Northern Hemisphere, southern Asia as far as central Malaysia and the Philippines

ECONOMIC USES: timber; also grown as ornamentals

▲ Male cones of the English yew appear in spring but remain for only a short time.

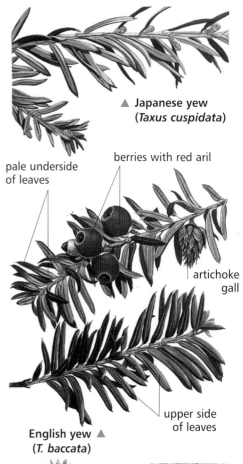

▲ Japanese yew (*Taxus cuspidata*)

pale underside of leaves

berries with red aril

artichoke gall

English yew ▲ (*T. baccata*)

upper side of leaves

A mature English yew ▲ and its scaly bark

for hedging; yew hedges are frequently tall, with smooth, vertical sides and flat tops.

There are also some popular ornamentals, and there are several varieties that differ in shape and in their leaves. 'Fastigiata,' or Irish yew, is a widely grown variety. It is a compact, column-shaped tree up to 33 feet (10 m) tall, with branches that grow upward, parallel to the trunk.

Japanese yew can grow into a column-shaped tree up to 65 feet (20 m). Cultivated varieties include some that grow as spreading shrubs. Japanese and English yews have been crossbred to produce a hybrid that combines the vigorous growth of the English yew with the hardiness of the Japanese. Many cultivated yews are varieties developed from this hybrid.

Western yew occurs naturally from British Columbia to California. It is a tree that grows to a height of 50 feet (15 m). Canada yew is a low shrub that is native to Canada and the northeastern United States. Canada yew has also been crossed with Japanese yew to produce a cultivated hybrid.

▲ Of all the species of yews, two are especially popular as ornamental plants: the English yew and Japanese yew. They have narrow leaves and seeds enclosed in a red, fleshy, cup-shaped aril.

See Also | *DISPERSAL OF FRUITS AND SEEDS* **2** *36* | *TIMBER* **5** *44* | *WHAT IS A CONIFER?* **8** *4* 👁

Glossary

Using the glossary Abbreviations: (adj.) adjective, (pl.) plural, (sing.) singular. Words set in SMALL CAPITALS *refer to related entries in the glossary.*

acid rain A form of air pollution by acids, mainly sulfuric and nitric, that are released by the burning of fossil fuels. The acids may be deposited directly onto plant surfaces or dissolved in mist, rain, or snow and deposited in solution onto plants or the ground.

acid soil A soil that is more acid than pure water (its pH is less than 7.0). A soil is considered very acid if its pH is less than 5.0.

alkaline soil A soil that is more alkaline than pure water (its pH is greater than 7.0). Soils are not usually considered strongly alkaline unless they have a pH between 8.0 and 10.0.

aphid A small, soft-bodied insect that feeds on plant sap. Greenfly and blackfly are aphids.

archegonium (*pl.* **archegonia**) An organ producing female sex cells.

aril A fleshy outer covering to a seed. The fleshy cup surrounding the seed of a yew TREE is an aril, and the arils surrounding nutmegs are dried to produce the spice called mace.

artichoke gall A close bunching of leaves on a yew TREE that is caused by an insect pest, the yew-gall midge.

balsam A semisolid mixture of RESIN and oils that evaporate readily, often with a characteristic odor.

bark The tissue that lies on the outside of the stem, branches, and roots of a TREE or SHRUB. The definition is sometimes confined to the outermost layer of dead cells and sometimes includes cells beneath this layer that are actively dividing.

bootlace fungus *See* HONEY FUNGUS.

bract An organ resembling a leaf that covers each scale on the CONE of a Douglas fir.

bristlecone pine The most long-lived TREE in the world. Some individuals are up to 5,000 years old.

buttress root A main TREE root that joins the trunk some distance above ground level. It grows away from the trunk at an angle, but remains attached to the trunk for the whole of its length, so looks like a buttress and helps support the TREE. Buttress roots are found on trees that grow in soft ground.

Canada balsam BALSAM made with RESIN from the balsam fir. It is used to attach cover slips to microscope slides and to fix together the elements from which complex lenses are made.

Canada pitch RESIN from the Canada hemlock that has been boiled in water, skimmed, and boiled a second time. It is used as a herbal medicine to treat mild skin irritations.

canker A plant disease in which tissue dies and is then surrounded by many layers of unspecialized cells. Cankers occur mainly on the trunks and branches of trees and shrubs. They are caused by fungal infections; as the fungus penetrates the plant it produces layers of protective tissue to isolate the infected region.

cedar-wood oil An oil obtained from the pencil cedar (in fact a juniper) and used in polishes and soap.

Chile nuts The edible seeds of the monkey puzzle TREE, or Chile pine.

chromosome A structure that contains genetic information. Shaped like a thread, it is made from a complex arrangement of proteins and DNA.

cone A group of closely packed, modified leaves surrounding a central axis that bears the reproductive structures of the plant. Male and female cones are distinct.

conifer A TREE that bears its seeds in CONES. Conifers are in the phylum Coniferophyta, which includes pines, firs, spruces, larches, hemlocks, Douglas firs, junipers, and yews.

cotyledon (seed leaf) The first leaf of a new plant. The seed contains one or more cotyledons. After germination PHOTOSYNTHESIS in the cotyledons sustains the plant until its true leaves appear.

cultivar A variety of a plant species that has been produced by agricultural or horticultural techniques, such as selective breeding, and that does not occur naturally. The word is a contraction of "cultivated variety."

deciduous Shed periodically. A deciduous TREE or SHRUB sheds all of its leaves at the end of the growing season.

diploid Having two copies of each CHROMOSOME in every cell.

embryo A young plant, after fertilization has occurred, when the cells have started to differentiate into particular structures.

endosperm A store of starch contained in the seed that sustains the young plant until it is able to obtain nutrients independently.

evergreen A TREE or SHRUB that bears leaves at all times of year. Although its leaves eventually die and are shed, they are not all shed at the same time. CONIFER leaves live from three to 10 years.

exine The tough outer coat of a POLLEN GRAIN.

fastigiate Growing with the branches pointing upward.

fir candle The central spine that remains after a silver fir CONE has released its seeds and disintegrated. The presence of fir candles is a sure indication that the TREE is a silver fir.

gametophyte The structure in which the HAPLOID reproductive cells are produced. It is the haploid generation in the life cycle of the plant.

gas exchange The movement of gases into and out of a plants through the leaf STOMATA.

generative cell The cell in a POLLEN GRAIN that divides to form two sperm cells.

haploid Having only one copy of each CHROMOSOME in every cell.

hard pine A species of pine trees made up of trees that produce much more RESIN than members of certain other species.

hardwood Wood from a broad-leaved TREE, such as oak, beech, or ash.

honey fungus (bootlace fungus) The most destructive of all fungal diseases, although most conifers are less susceptible than broad-leaved trees. The fungus infects the stump of a felled TREE, then spreads through the soil as long, black threads resembling bootlaces that will enter through the smallest crack in the root of a tree. It then spreads throughout the tree and rots the whole of it.

hybrid An individual produced by parents that belong to different sub-species or species.

hybridization Sexual reproduction by two individuals that belong to different subspecies or species. Their offspring is a HYBRID.

integument A protective layer of tissue that surrounds an OVULE completely, except for the MICROPYLE.

intine The thin, inner coat of a POLLEN GRAIN.

knee A vertical loop that rises upward from a main root running horizontally just below the surface of WATERLOGGED ground. The part of the loop that is exposed to the air has many small pores through which air can enter the root.

larch manna A sweet white substance that is exuded from larch leaves. People once rubbed it on the chest to relieve bronchial complaints.

living fossil A plant that is almost identical to species that lived millions of years ago and that are known only from fossils. The dawn redwood is a living fossil.

megaspore A HAPLOID structure that develops into the female GAMETOPHYTE.

megaspore mother cell The cell from which the female reproductive cells develop.

meiosis (reduction division) A DIPLOID cell divides twice to produce four HAPLOID cells, each with half the number of CHROMOSOMES of the parent cell.

micropyle A small opening at the tip of an OVULE through which the pollen tube enters the NUCELLUS.

microsporangium (pollen sac) The structure that produces HAPLOID MICROSPORES (POLLEN GRAINS). In seed-producing plants the pollen grain is the microsporangium.

microspore A HAPLOID spore that develops into a male GAMETOPHYTE.

microspore mother cell *See* POLLEN MOTHER CELL.

microsporophyll A modified leaf that bears a MICROSPORANGIUM.

nucellus A mass of unspecialized cells in the OVULE. It contains the EMBRYO sac and egg cell.

nurse tree A fast-growing TREE that is planted beside a slower-growing tree to protect it from the wind. By the time the slower-growing tree is big enough to be shaded by it, the nurse tree is ready to be felled.

ovule The structure inside the ovary that contains the egg cell inside an EMBRYO sac, with the tissues that nourish and protect it. After fertilization the ovule will develop into a seed.

permafrost A layer of ground that is permanently frozen. To become permafrost, the ground must remain frozen for at least two consecutive winters and the summer between.

phloem Tissue composed of tubular cells, arranged end to end, through which sugars are transported from the leaves to every other part of the plant.

photosynthesis The process by which green plants manufacture sugar from carbon dioxide and water, using sunlight energy.

plantation A group of trees, usually of the same species, that are grown as a commercial crop.

plumule The part of the EMBRYO that will become the stem of the plant.

pollen grain A small structure that contains HAPLOID male cell nuclei.

pollen mother cell (microspore mother cell) A cell that divides by MEIOSIS to produce pollen grains.

pollen sac *See* MICROSPORANGIUM.

pollination The transfer of pollen grains from the MICROSPORANGIUM to the OVULE.

proembryo The new plant after the ZYGOTE has divided but before its cells have differentiated to form particular structures.

prothallial cell A small cell that is formed together with the GENERATIVE CELL when the MICROSPORE divides for the first time. The prothallial cell undergoes no further divisions.

radicle The part of the EMBRYO that will become the root of the plant.

reduction division *See* MEIOSIS.

resin A sticky liquid, produced from a wound by conifers when injured. It is insoluble in water but soluble in alcohol. It hardens on exposure to air forming a solid, or semisolid, covering that protects the wound and prevents it from becoming infected.

resin duct A channel that runs in the XYLEM and leaves of most conifers and inside which RESIN is produced.

respiration The process through which cells obtain energy. Food (in the form of sugar) is broken down by a sequence of chemical reactions into progressively simpler substances; finally, carbon and hydrogen are oxidized using oxygen absorbed from the air. Carbon dioxide and water vapor are released as waste products.

rosin *See* TURPENTINE.

seed leaf *See* COTYLEDON.

shrub A woody plant that is less than 33 feet (10 m) tall and that divides near ground level into several main stems, but has no single trunk. It lives for several years and does not die back at the end of each growing season.

soft pine A species of pine trees made up of trees that produce much less RESIN than members of certain other species.

softwood Wood from a coniferous TREE, such as pine, hemlock, fir, or spruce.

sporophyte A plant during the generation in its life cycle when its cells are DIPLOID. In conifers the sporophyte is the dominant generation; it is the familiar plant.

stomata (*sing.* **stoma**) Pores in the surface of leaves (and sometimes also stems) through which GAS EXCHANGE takes place. Carbon dioxide for PHOTOSYNTHESIS and oxygen for RESPIRATION enter the plant, and water vapor, carbon dioxide, and oxygen leave it.

suspensor A structure that attaches the EMBRYO to the tissue of the parent plant. The suspensor is made from cells that differentiate from the PROEMBRYO.

swamp An area of land that remains covered by shallow water throughout the year.

taiga The broad belt of forest that stretches across northern Eurasia from Scandinavia to the Pacific, in which the predominant trees are conifers.

tanbark The BARK of hemlock trees, which is used for TANNING leather.

tanning The process of converting an animal skin into leather by treating it with certain chemicals, especially tannin.

topiary The art of training and pruning trees and shrubs into sculptural shapes. Yew is an especially popular subject for topiary because of the density of its foliage.

tracheid A type of cell found in XYLEM tissue in vascular plants other than flowering plants. Long, narrow, and with tapering ends, tracheids overlap adjacent cells. There are perforations, mainly in the end walls, through which water can flow.

tree A woody plant that is more than 33 feet (10 m) tall and usually has one main trunk (although some trees have several). It lives for several years and does not die back at the end of each growing season.

tube cell In POLLEN GRAINS the cell that develops into the pollen tube but disappears after fertilization.

tundra The vegetation that is found in latitudes beyond the treeline. It consists of grasses, sedges, mosses, lichens, and low SHRUBS.

turpentine An oil (C_6H_{16}) that is obtained by distilling RESIN. The residue, called rosin, is used in making lacquers, varnishes, and paints.

waterlogged Saturated, so that all the small spaces between soil particles have been filled by water, expelling all the air.

whitewood The wood of spruce trees, so called because it is very pale in color.

xylem Tissue composed of tubular cells, arranged end to end, through which water and dissolved nutrients are transported from the roots to every other part of the plant.

zygote The cell that is formed by the fusion of the male and female reproductive cells before it has undergone division. When it divides, it becomes a PROEMBRYO.

Scientific Names

In this set common names have been used wherever possible. Listed below are the plants mentioned in this volume for which scientific names have not already been given. See Volume 1, page 7 for further detail on the naming of plants.

Alaska cypress *Chamaecyparis nootkatensis*
Aleppo pine *Pinus halepensis*
alligator juniper *Juniperus deppeana*
American arborvitae *Thuja occidentalis*
arborvitae *Thuja* species
Ashe juniper *Juniperus ashei*
Atlantic cedar *Cedrus atlantica*
Austrian pine *Pinus nigra*
baker cypress *Cupressus bakeri*
bald cypress *Taxodium distichum*
balsam fir *Abies balsamea*
beach pine *Pinus contorta*
Bermuda juniper *Juniperus bermudiana*
Bhutan pine *Pinus wallichiana*
big tree (also called Sierra redwood) *Sequoiadendron giganteum*
black spruce *Picea mariana*
bristlecone pine *Pinus longaeva*
bunya-bunya *Araucaria bidwillii*
Canada hemlock *Tsuga canadensis*
Canada yew *Taxus canadensis*
Carolina hemlock *Tsuga caroliniana*
Cascade fir *Abies amabilis*
Caucasian spruce *Picea orientalis*
cedar of Goa *Cupressus lusitanica*
cedar of Lebanon *Cedrus libani*
cedars *Cedrus* species
Chinese Douglas fir *Pseudotsuga sinensis*
Chinese hemlock *Tsuga chinensis*
Chinese juniper *Juniperus chinensis*
cluster pine *Pinus pinaster*
coast redwood *Sequoia sempervirens*
Colorado spruce *Picea pungens*
common juniper *Juniperus communis*
Corsican pine *Pinus nigra* var. *maritima*
Cyprus cedar *Cedrus brevifolia*
Daurian larch *Larix gmelini*
dawn redwood *Metasequoia glyptostroboides*
deodar *Cedrus deodara*
Douglas firs *Pseudotsuga* species
Douglas fir *Pseudotsuga menziesii*
Dunkeld larch *Larix* x *eurolepis*
eastern white pine *Pinus strobus*
Engelmann spruce *Picea engelmannii*

English yew *Taxus baccata*
European larch *Larix decidua*
European silver fir *Abies alba*
firs *Abies* species
Formosa cypress *Chamaecyparis formosensis*
foxtail pine *Pinus balfouriana*
Fraser fir *Abies fraseri*
giant fir *Abies grandis*
Gowen cypress *Cupressus goveniana*
Greek fir *Abies cephalonica*
Guadalupe cypress *Cupressus guadalupensis*
hemlocks (firs) *Tsuga* species
hickory pine *Pinus aristata*
Himalayan spruce *Picea smithiana*
Hinoki cypress *Chamaecyparis obtusa*
hoop pine *Araucaria cunninghamii*
Irish yew *Taxus baccata* 'Fastigiata'
Italian cypress *Cupressus sempervirens*
Japanese arborvitae *Thuja standishii*
Japanese Douglas fir *Pseudotsuga japonica*
Japanese larch *Larix kaempferi*
Japanese yew *Taxus cuspidata*
junipers *Juniperus* species
klinki pine *Araucaria hunsteinii*
Korean arborvitae *Thuja koraiensis*
Korean fir *Abies koreana*
larches *Larix* species
large-coned Douglas fir *Pseudotsuga macrocarpa*
Lawson cypress *Chamaecyparis lawsoniana*
Leyland cypress x *Cupressocyparis leylandii*
loblolly pine *Pinus taeda*
lodgepole pine *Pinus contorta* var. *latifolia*
maples *Acer* species
monkey puzzle tree *Araucaria araucana*
Monterey cypress *Cupressus macrocarpa*
Monterey pine *Pinus radiata*
Montezuma cypress *Taxodium mucronatum*
mountain hemlock *Tsuga mertensiana*
noble fir *Abies procera*

Nordmann fir *Abies nordmanniana*
Norfolk Island pine *Araucaria heterophylla*
northern Japanese hemlock *Tsuga diversifolia*
Norway spruce *Picea abies*
oriental arborvitae *Platycladus orientalis*
Pacific fir *Abies amabilis*
paraná pine *Araucaria angustifolia*
pencil cedar *Juniperus virginiana*
pines *Pinus* species
pitch pine *Pinus palustris*
ponderosa pine *Pinus ponderosa*
red fir *Abies magnifica*
red spruce *Picea rubens*
redwoods *Sequoia sempervirens* and *Sequoiadendron giganteum*
Rocky Mountain juniper *Juniperus scopulorum*
rough-barked Arizona cypress *Cupressus arizonica*
Scotch pine *Pinus sylvestris*
Serbian spruce *Picea omorika*
Siberian larch *Larix sibirica*
Sichuan arborvitae *Thuja sutchuenensis*
Sikkim larch *Larix griffithiana*
Sitka spruce *Picea sitchensis*
smooth cypress *Cupressus glabra*
southern Japanese hemlock *Tsuga sieboldii*
Spanish fir *Abies pinsapo*
spruces *Picea* species
stone pine *Pinus pinea*
sugar pine *Pinus lambertiana*
swamp cypresses *Taxodium* species
tamarack *Larix laricina*
western hemlock *Tsuga heterophylla*
western juniper *Juniperus occidentalis*
western larch *Larix occidentalis*
western red cedar *Thuja plicata*
western yew *Taxus brevifolia*
white cedar *Chamaecyparis thyoides*
white cedar *Thuja occidentalis*
white fir *Abies concolor*
white spruce *Picea glauca*
yews *Taxus* species

Set Index

Major entries are shown by bold key words with relevant page numbers underlined. Bold numbers indicate volumes. Italic numbers indicate picture captions.

Scientific names of plants cited under common names in this Index are to be found at the end of each individual volume.

coleorhiza 2: *29*
coleus 1: *43*, 10: *43*
collenchyma 1: *19*, 21
colloid 7: 9
colonial bent 4: 23
colonization 2: 24, 32, 4: 22–24, *23*, 7: 12, 16, *16*
recolonization 4: 44–45
see also pioneer species
color 1: 14, 9: 6
carnivorous plants 3: 36
chloroplasts 1: 14, 21, 30, *39*, 43, 3: 6
dinoflagellates 6: 19
etiolation 3: 22, *23*
ferns 7: 34, 36
flowers 2: 4, 9, 10–11, *10–11*, 19, 23
fruit 2: 32–33, *32*, 38
genetic dominance 2: 42–45, *42*, *43*, *45*
leaves 1: 42–43, *42*, 3: 32
mineral deficiency 3: 30–32, *30*, *31*
sepals 2: 5, 9
ultraviolet 2: *10*, 19
variegation 1: *43*
see also pigment
columbine 2: 33, 10: *9*, 10
columnella 6: 33, *33*
Commelinaceae 9: 36–37
community 4: 8
competing plants 4: 28–31, 33
conceptacle 6: 27, *27*
cone 1: *5*, 6: *4*, 8: 4, 6, *7*, 8, 10, *11*, 15, 19, 27, 31, 39, 46
club mosses 7: 23–24, *24*
cycads 7: 44, *45*
horsetails 7: 30
Welwitschia 7: 46
see also conifer; gymnosperm
conidiophore 6: 45, *45*
conidium 6: 45, *45*
conifer 16, 1: *5*, 43, 48, 49, 3: 45–46, 4: 26, 34, 43, 5: 46, 6: *4*, 9, 7: 18, 8: 4–9, *4*
boreal forest 4: 36, 38
coastal coniferous biome 4: 36, 38
evolution 7: 47
life cycle 6: *11*, 8: 6–7, *7*
pollen 2: 16
conservation 1: 35, 4: 44–48, 5: 46, 47, 48, 9: 27
acid rain 8: 17, *17*
forests 5: 46, 47, 8: 17, 20
global warming 7: 19
grasslands 9: 15
and horticulture 5: 48
kelp forests 6: 28
nature reserves 10: 10
orchids 9: 18
palm species 9: 32
peat bogs 7: 15
use of fertilizers 3: 33
Convention on International Trade in Endangered Species (CITES) 4: 48
convolvulus 9: *5*

copper 3: 31
copra 9: 30
coral 6: 19, 20
coral (fungus) 6: 39
clustered 6: *38*
pestle-shaped 6: *38*
coral spot 6: 47, *47*
coral tree 10: *30*
coralline algae 6: 20–21, *20*
Cordaites 7: *21*
coriander 5: *37*, 38, 10: 38
cork 1: 24, 26, 47, 48, *49*, 3: *17*, 5: 44, 10: 12
cork oak *see* oak
cork tree 10: 36
corm 1: 23, *23*, 32–33, 34–35, *35*, 36, *36*, 37, 2: 15, 9: 22, 28, *29*
adventitious roots 1: 23
vegetative reproduction 2: 46–48, *47*, 3: 49
corn (maize) 1: 22, 26, *26*, 31, 32, 45, 2: 29, 30, 33, 5: 5, *12*, 13, 32, 33, 41, 9: 10, 12
photosynthesis 3: 7
corolla 9: *4*
corona 2: 9, 9: 24–25, *25*, 26
cortex 1: *19*, 24, 25, *25*, 30, 31, 32, 47–48, 6: 28, 9: 9
Corybas bicalcarata 9: *19*
corymb 2: *13*, 9: 44, 10: 20, *21*
Cosmarium 6: 24, *24*
costmary 5: *37*
cotoneaster 10: 28, *29*
cotton 2: 36, 5: 31, 34, *34*, *35*
cotton grass 9: *15*
cotyledon 1: 44–45, *44*, *45*, 2: *27*, 29–30, *29*, *33*, 8: 7, *7*, 9: 6, *7*, 8, 10: 4
dicotyledon *see* dicotyledon
edible 10: 20
monocotyledon *see* monocotyledon
cow parsnip 10: *39*
cow wheat 3: 41
cowbane 10: 38
cowslip, American 10: 24, *25*
cranberry 5: *8*, 10: 22
cremocarp 2: *34*
creosote bush 3: 44–45, 4: 38, 43
cress, garden 10: 20
cristae 3: 11, *11*
crocus 1: *23*, 33, 35, *36*, 2: 46–47, *47*, 3: 20, 5: 36, 49, 9: 28, *29*
autumn *see* autumn crocus
crop rotation 3: 35, 6: 40
crops
fruit 5: 8–11
oil 5: 30–31
root 5: 26–29
starch 5: 32–33
sugar 5: 32–33
crossing over 2: 41
croton 5: 31, 10: *35*
Crowea saligna 10: *37*
cruciform 10: 20, *20*, *21*
cryptomonad 6: 14

cucumber 1: 24, 5: 21–22, *22*, *23*
family 10: 18–19, *19*
wild 10: *19*
cucumber tree 10: 7
Cucurbitaceae 10: 18–19
cultivar 1: 7
cultivation 4: 45–47, 5: 4–6
shifting *see* slash-and-burn farming
see also domestication; horticulture
cumin 5: 38, 10: 38
cup fungus 6: *30*, 44–47, *44–47*
lichen 6: 48–49
recurved 6: *46*
scarlet 6: *46*
Cupressus 8: 40–43
Cupressocyparis 8: 40–43
cupule 10: *13*
currant 5: 8
cuticle 1: 21, 30, 32, 38, 39, 43, 3: 6, 27, 44, 46, 48, 6: 8, 7: 24
cutting 2: 49
cyanobacteria 3: 35, 4: 17, 19, 6: 5, *6*, 12–13, *13*, 21, 7: 38
evolution 1: *5*
hornworts 7: 16
lichens 6: 48–49
cyathium 10: 34
cycad 1: *5*, 6: *4*, 8, 11, 7: 18, 44–45, *45*
Cycadophyta 7: 44–45
cyclamen 4: 45, 47, 10: 24, *25*
Cymbidium 9: *18*
cyme 9: 20, *21*, 28, *29*, 36, *37*, 10: 10, *16*, *17*, 34, 44
cymose inflorescence 2: *13*
Cyperaceae 9: 42–43
cypress 8: 4, 40–43, *41*, *42*, 43
Alaska cedar 8: 42, 43, *43*
Arizona 8: 41
baker 8: 41
bald *see* bald cypress
cedar of Goa 8: 41–42
false 8: 40, 42–43
Formosa 8: 42–43
Gowen 8: 41
Guadalupe 8: 41
Hinoki 8: 42–43
Italian (funeral) 8: 40, *41*, *42*
Lawson 8: 42, *43*
Leyland 8: 40, *41*, 43, *43*
Monterey 8: 40, *41*
Montezuma (Mexican) *see* Montezuma cypress
swamp 8: 36–37
true 8: 40–42
white cedar 8: 42
cypsela 2: *35*
Cytinus 3: 40, *41*
cytokinin 3: 13–14, *13*, 16
cytoplasm 1: *13*, 14, 15, 3: *24*, 6: 6, 8, 16, 24, 30
cytoskeleton 1: 15

D

daffodil 1: 33, *34*, 36, 37, 2: 5, *7*, 9, 27, 47, 5: 49, 9: 10
family 9: 24–27, *24–27*
hoop-petticoat 9: *25*
sea 9: 25, 26
dahlia 1: *23*, 24, 3: *43*, 10: 46, 48
daisy 1: 24, 31, 37, 2: 9, *13*, 10: 46, 48
common 10: 46, *46*
damaged plants *see* wounded or damaged plants
Damasonium 9: 46
damson 5: 8, 10, 10: 28, *29*
dandelion 1: 22, 2: 33, *35*, *37*, 5: 41, 9: 6, 10: 46
dasheen *see* taro
date palm 2: 18, 34, 5: 10, *32*, 33, 9: 30, *32*
day flower 9: *37*
day length, reactions to 2: 30, 3: 21, 42
day-neutral species 3: 21
dead man's finger 6: *47*
deadly nightshade 4: 31, 5: 42, *43*, 10: 41
death cap 6: 40
decable species 1: 37, 43, 3: 42, 4: 36, 39–40, *40*, 43
triggering shedding 3: 12, 15, 16, *17*, 42
decomposer 4: 11, 14–15, 6: 13, 30, 32, 34, 41
defense mechanisms 3: 30, 4: 28–31, 28, 29
deficiency diseases 3: 30–31, *30*, *31*
dehiscing 2: *35*, 7: *6*
delphinium 2: 33, *35*, 10: 10
Dendrobium pulchellum 9: *17*
denitrification 4: *16*, 17
deodar 8: 31, *31*
deoxyribonucleic acid (DNA) 1: 14, 16, 2: 40–45, 3: 32, 34, 6: 5
bacteria 6: 12–13
meiosis 2: 40–41, *40–41*, 45
Derbesia 6: 24
desert biome 1: 24, 32, 34, 43, *43*, 45, 2: 30, 3: 31, 42–43, 44–46, *45*, 4: 20, 34, 36, 38, 43, 10: 14, 34
semi-desert 4: 36, 38
desmid 6: 24
destroying angel 6: 40
detritus 4: *9*
devil's guts (thread) *see* dodder
devil's tobacco pouch 6: 40
diatom 6: 14, 18–19, *18*, *19*
dichasium 2: *13*, 10: 16, *17*
dichotomous branching 9: *31*, 32
dicotyledon (dicot) 1: *5*, 31, 6: *4*, 9: 8, *9*, 10: 4, *4*
flowers 9: 9, 10: 4
leaves 10: 4
roots 1: 25, 10: 4
stems 1: *30*, 31–32, 10: 4
Dicotyledones 10: 4–5

Dieffenbachia 9: 38
differentiation 1: 46, 3: 13
diffusion 3: 24, *24*, 27, 32–33
dill 5: *37*, 38, 10: 38
dinoflagellate 6: 14, 15, 19, *19*
Dinomastigota 6: 19
dioecious 2: 18
diploid 5: *6*, 6: 10, 23, 7: 6, 10, 9: 6
dipterocarp 5: *47*
Disa hamatopetala 9: *19*
disk floret *see* floret
Distichia 9: 45
division, cell *see* cell
DNA *see* deoxyribonucleic acid
dodder 3: 40, *40*
domestication 5: 4–6, *4–6*, 16, 48–49
dormancy 1: *28*, 2: 28, 3: 14–15, 42, *43*, 44, 4: 30, 38, 44, 48, 6: 13, 7: 37
Douglas fir 8: 24–25
drepanium 2: *13*, 9: 44, *45*
drip tip 1: 43, 4: 40
dropper 2: 48
drought 1: 43, 45, 3: 14–15, 29, 42–43, 44–46, *44*, *45*, 4: 38, 42, 7: 10, 27, 41, 46–47, *46*, 8: 4, 6
drupe 2: 34, *34*, 9: 31, 10: 22, 27, 29, 36
dry rot 6: 39
duckmeat *see* duckweed
duckweed 3: 48, 7: *36*, 9: 10, 48,
common 9: *49*
family 9: 48–49, *48*, *49*
greater 9: *49*
least 9: *49*
dulse 6: 21
dumb cane 1: 33, 43, 9: 38
Dunaliella 6: 22
durian 5: *10*, 11

E

E. coli 6: *12*
earthstar 6: 37, 38–39
collared 6: *39*
ebony 5: 44, 46
Cretan 4: *33*
Echinocereus 3: 45
ecology 4: 4, 6
ecosystem 4: 4, 6, *6*, 4–11
Ectocarpus 6: 27
eddo *see* taro
eelgrass 2: 25
egg *see* ovum
eggplant 5: 21, *22*, 10: 40
elater 7: *6*, *7*, 16
elder 2: *15*
electrical signals 3: 20–21, *20*, 27–28, 38–39
elephant's tongue 7: 41
eliasome 2: 39
elm 2: *35*, 36, 6: 31, 9: *5*
embryo 1: 44–45, *45*, 2: 4, 26, 27, 29, *29*, 33, 38, 40, 8: 7, *7*, 9: 6, *7*, 9
emergent 4: 40

Further Reading   Volume 8: Conifers

Biomes of the World: Temperate Forests by Michael Allaby. Grolier Educational, 1999.

Dirr's Hardy Trees and Shrubs by Michael A. Dirr. Timber Press, 1997

Ecosystem: Temperate Forests by Michael Allaby. Facts on File, 1999.

National Audubon Society Field Guide to Trees. 1: Western Region; 2: Eastern Region. by Elbert L. Little. Alfred A. Knopf, 1995

Natural Woodland: Ecology and Conservation in Northern Temperate Regions by George F. Peterken. Cambridge University Press, 1996.

Useful website addresses

The American Conifer Society
www.pacificrim.net/~bydesign/acs3.html

Conifer Trees
www.planet-pets.com/treecnfr.htm

Cypress (*Cupressus*)
www.orst.edu/instruct/for241/con/cyprgen.html

Douglas-fir (*Pseudotsuga*)
www.orst.edu/instruct/for241/con/dfgen.html

False Cedars (*Calocedrus, Thuja, Chamaecyparis*)
www.orst.edu/instruct/for241/con/cedrgen.html

Forestry: The Great American Coniferous Forest by Steve Nix
forestry.about.com/education/forestry/libra.../aa071899.htm

Giant sequoia (*Sequoiadendron giganteum*)
www.orst.edu/instruct/for241/con/giseqgen.html

Gymnosperm Database
home.earthlink.net/~earlecj/

Hemlocks (*Tsuga*)
www.orst.edu/instruct/for241/con/hmlckgen.html

Introduction to the Conifers: Not Just for Christmas Anymore
www.ucmp.berkeley.edu/seedplants/conifers/conifers.html

Larches (*Larix*)
www.orst.edu/instruct/for241/con/lrchgen.html

North America's Top 100 Trees by Steve Nix
forestry.about.com/education/forestry/libra.../blcondex.htm

Pines (*Pinus*)
www.orst.edu/instruct/for241/con/pinegen.html

Trees of the Pacific Northwest
www.orst.edu/instruct/for241/

True Firs (*Abies*)
www.orst.edu/instruct/for241/con/trfirgen.html

Yews (*Taxus*)
www.orst.edu/instruct/for241/con/yewgen.html

(on conifers):
www.albion.edu/plants/CONIFAMS.HTM

Picture Credits   Volume 8: Conifers